RETHINKING TEACHER PREPARATION PROGRAM DESIGN

This book provides a framework, concrete examples, and tools for designing a high quality, academically-robust preservice teacher preparation program that empowers teachers with the depth of professional knowledge and the skills required to become adaptable, responsive K-12 teachers ready to engage with diverse groups of students, and to achieve consistent learning outcomes.

Renowned teacher educators Etta R. Hollins and Connor K. Warner present a systematic approach for developing a teacher preparation program characterized by coherence, continuity, consistency, integrity, and trustworthiness, as well as one that is firmly grounded in collaboration between faculty, community members, and other school practitioners.

This book offers an evidence-based roadmap relevant for teacher educators, administrators, scholars, agencies at the state and national levels, and any organization that serves teacher educators.

Etta R. Hollins is Professor Emeritus and Ewing Marion Kauffman Endowed Chair for Urban Teacher Education at the University of Missouri-Kansas City, USA.

Connor K. Warner is an Assistant Professor of Education in the Urban Institute for Teacher Education at the University of Utah, Salt Lake City, USA.

RETHINKING TEACHER PREPARATION PROGRAM DESIGN

Etta R. Hollins and Connor K. Warner

Routledge
Taylor & Francis Group

NEW YORK AND LONDON

First published 2021
by Routledge
605 Third Avenue, New York, NY 10158

and by Routledge
2 Park Square, Milton Park, Abingdon, Oxon, OX14 4RN

Routledge is an imprint of the Taylor & Francis Group, an informa business

Library of Congress Cataloging-in-Publication Data
Names: Hollins, Etta R., 1942- author. | Warner, Connor K., author.
Title: Rethinking teacher preparation program design / Etta R. Hollins,
Connor K. Warner.
Description: New York, N.Y. : Routledge, 2021. | Includes bibliographical
references.
Identifiers: LCCN 2020052993 (print) | LCCN 2020052994 (ebook) |
ISBN 9780367713904 (paperback) | ISBN 9780367713935 (hardback) |
ISBN 9781003150633 (ebook)
Subjects: LCSH: Teachers--Training of--United States. | Education--Study
and teaching (Higher)--United States.
Classification: LCC LB1715 .H636 2021 (print) | LCC LB1715 (ebook) |
DDC 370.71/1--dc23
LC record available at https://lccn.loc.gov/2020052993
LC ebook record available at https://lccn.loc.gov/2020052994

ISBN: 978-0-367-71393-5 (hbk)
ISBN: 978-0-367-71390-4 (pbk)
ISBN: 978-1-003-15063-3 (ebk)

Typeset in Bembo
by Taylor & Francis Books

This book is dedicated to accomplished teaching that supports each student in meeting the highest developmental potential, and the teacher educators and administrators that promote it. We give special recognition to Roy D Warner for his educational leadership and inspiration.

CONTENTS

ILLUSTRATIONS

Figures

Tables

PREFACE

The education of teachers in the United States needs to be turned upside down. To prepare effective teachers for 21st Century classrooms, teacher education must shift away from a norm which emphasizes academic preparation and course work loosely linked to school-based experiences. Rather, it must move to programs that are fully grounded in clinical practice and interwoven with academic content and professional courses.

(NCATE Blue Ribbon Panel Report, 2010)

This book presents an approach for designing academically based preservice teacher preparation grounded in clinical practice as called for in the NCATE Blue Ribbon Panel Report (2010) and the AACTE Clinical Practice Commission (2018). The Blue Ribbon Panel identified ten design principles for clinically based teacher preparation and the AACTE commission presented a conceptual model and ten proclamations. These design principles and program attributes are addressed in the approach presented in this book.

The discussion in this book represents teaching as a profession wherein practitioners have a shared knowledge base, clearly defined goals supported by established practices and procedures that generate predictable outcomes; and agreed upon protocols for addressing problems of practice. Creativity and innovation are aspects of problem solving, rather than disruptions of established practices and procedures for achieving predictable outcomes. Teaching is defined as an interpretive process that involves deep knowledge and continuous observation, analysis, and responsiveness to the interrelationship among learner characteristics, learning, subject matter, pedagogy, and learning outcomes. Research on teaching investigates specific problems of classroom practice, professional preparation, and develops new practices and procedures for testing and validation.

Preservice teacher preparation models the professional practices and procedures for teaching. In addition to the shared knowledge base for teaching, teacher educators have a shared knowledge base, practices and procedures for the process of learning to teach. Teacher preparation involves developing the deep knowledge and habits of mind associated with teaching as an interpretive process. Further, the design of teacher preparation programs is responsive to existing and new knowledge in the field, local and national needs, and state and national standards for the teaching profession and for teacher preparation.

The Aim of this Book

The aim of this book is to contribute to shared understanding of professional preparation for teaching that will advance teaching practices with predictable outcomes for P-12 students. This means consistently preparing teachers whose students from all subgroups regularly meet expectations for subject matter and grade level. This type of teacher preparation requires a program design characterized by coherence, continuity, and consistency; a stable curriculum that can be validated over time; and program practices that develop the essential knowledge, skills, and habits of mind. Coherence is the interconnectedness among the parts of a teacher preparation program that forms the basis for integrity and trustworthiness. Consistency exists when course objectives and assignments, and the relationship among courses and between courses and clinical experiences remain stable over time and across faculty. Changes in course objectives, assignments, and related clinical experiences require faculty consensus. Continuity refers to the developmental sequencing of courses and clinical experiences across the teacher preparation program.

The professional preparation of teachers is a preeminent concern because teaching is essential for developing the academic and intellectual resources required for leaders, scholars, researchers, professionals, and highly technical and service occupations that support the quality of life in the society. Presently, there are shortages in the United States in occupations and professions requiring high levels of knowledge and preparation in mathematics and science. These shortages have resulted in dependance on talent from other nations. However, federal legislation limits the number of H-1B visas for foreign specialty workers to 65,000 annually with another 20,000 for those foreign nationals earning advanced degrees from institutions of higher education in the United States. In 2013, there were more than 460,000 foreign nationals on H-1B visas employed in the United States in high paying specialty positions requiring advanced degrees for which US citizens were not qualified and available (USCIS, 2018).

The shortages of academic and intellectual resources in areas related to science, technology, and mathematics (STEM) are expected to grow exponentially with advances in technology. These shortages result from the academic preparation and performance of students in elementary and secondary schools. Data from the National Assessment of Educational Progress (NAEP) reveal that in 2019, only

35% of fourth graders scored proficient or above in reading, 34% of eighth graders, and 37% of twelfth graders. In mathematics, 41% of fourth graders scored at proficient or above, 34% of eighth graders, and 25% of twelfth graders. There is considerably variation across subgroups, states, school districts, and schools. However, nationally, not a single subgroup had 50% of twelfth graders score at proficient or above in reading or mathematics. This low level of academic performance in elementary and secondary schools leaves too many students unprepared for the rigorous demands of college level study in mathematics and science.

According to a report by Barry & Dannenberg (2016):

> Contrary to common belief, remedial education is a widespread phenomenon not at all confined to low-income students or community colleges. It affects a broad swath of students, including those from middle-, upper-middle, and high-income families, as well as a broad swath of colleges.

The findings from this study indicate that among first year entering college freshmen enrolled in non-credit remedial courses include, 57% of students in public 2-year colleges, 31% of students in public four-year colleges, and 12% of students in elite private colleges and universities. First year remedial students are 74% more likely to drop out of college than their non-remedial peers, and those that remain in college take a full year longer to graduate than their non-remedial peers. This represents a significant financial burden for families and a significant loss of academic and intellectual resources for the United States.

Approach and Organization of this Book

The underperformance of elementary and secondary school students that results in remedial coursework for significant numbers of entering college freshmen indicates a need for rethinking teaching practices and teacher preparation. This book presents an approach to rethinking teaching and teacher preparation by:

- (re)conceptualizing teaching and teacher preparation as academically based, and teaching as an interpretive practice/process;
- instituting coherence, continuity, consistency, and trustworthiness as quality indicators in the design of teacher preparation programs;
- providing a conceptual framework based on the interrelationship between conceptual and structural elements; and
- identifying practices and procedures for program design that include collaboration, program explication, course alignment and sequencing, integrated and authentic clinical experiences, and monitoring and assessing progress.

In the approach to preservice teacher preparation presented in this book, academic coursework and clinical experiences are correlated and integrated to facilitate professional knowledge and skills related to the application to practice in a teaching cycle and learning cycle that enable continuous analysis of instruction, the observation of students' responses, and the ability to adapt learning experiences to ensure that students meet expectations for grade level and subject matter.

Each chapter in this book addresses an essential aspect in the design for academically based teacher preparation. The chapters are organized to elaborate a program design framework that consists of conceptual and structural elements that are interrelated, and to delineate the practices, protocols, and tools that support each element. The process of learning to teach occurs within the program framework. Each chapter is supported by research, theory, and practice. Examples of the application to practice are provided and, where appropriate, procedures and tools are included.

In Chapter 1, academically based teacher preparation is presented as a meticulously designed approach grounded in the most reliable research, theory, and evidence from practice available; and that employs continuous data gathering and analysis for validation and improvement of practices, outcomes, and impact. Academically based teacher preparation programs include central and instrumental characteristics. Central characteristics include coherence, continuity, consistency, and trustworthiness. Instrumental characteristics include collaboration, interrelatedness of conceptual and structural elements, and systematic data collection. The central characteristics are program quality indicators. Instrumental characteristics are essential for program development, continuous improvement, and meeting the expectations of the quality indicators. Clinical experiences that provide opportunities for observation, documentation, analysis, and application of academic knowledge to practice in authentic settings serving students from diverse cultural and experiential backgrounds are an essential feature of academically based teacher preparation.

Collaboration among teacher educators and with practitioners and other stakeholders is essential for developing a reliable knowledge base for teaching and teacher preparation, and for designing teacher preparation programs that prepare competent teachers for P-12 schools. In Chapter 2, collaboration among teacher educators involves teamwork and a consensus generating process. Collaboration among teacher educators and with practitioners and other stakeholders involves clarifying shared goals, individual and collective responsibilities, and the official policies, regulations, and mandates influencing participants. The leadership for teacher preparation provides the context, information, and tools that enable and support collaboration among participants, access to the knowledge distributed among participants, consensus building, collaborative teamwork, and the development of a community of practice. Such collaboration produces mutual and reciprocal benefits for all participants and contributes to improving learning outcomes for schools and the quality of life in communities.

The teacher preparation program design framework presented in Chapter 3 includes conceptual elements and structural elements. The conceptual elements include a philosophical stance, a theoretical perspective on learning to teach, professional knowledge and skills, and epistemic practices. The structural elements include admission practices, the arrangement and relationship among courses and clinical experiences, assessment of candidates' professional knowledge and skills, and program evaluation. The conceptual and structural elements in the program are interconnected, complementary in function, and supported by correlated practices and protocols. The interconnectedness of the conceptual and structural elements is foundational in the program development and renewal process. This framework supports the central and instrumental characteristics of academically based teacher preparation discussed in Chapter 1.

The program explication process presented in Chapter 4 is for examining or developing the contours of the knowledge base for teaching and teacher preparation during program renewal or program development. The contours of the knowledge base are generated from an understanding of the best available knowledge in the field, conditions and needs in schools and communities, and state and national standards and requirements. This approach ensures that the contours of the knowledge base are consistent with the conceptual and structural elements of the teacher preparation program. The initial representation of the knowledge base is in brief descriptions of courses or modules and related clinical experiences. In program renewal, this process can involve revising, reorganizing, or replacing courses and creating new courses. Essential tools used in facilitating the program explication process include a program explication document, basic knowledge base framework, source documents for program authorization and approval, and a program approval process schedule. The preliminary knowledge base developed during the program explication process is elaborated in the course alignment process described in the next chapter.

In Chapter 5, course alignment is an approach to constructing a knowledge base for teaching and teacher preparation characterized by coherence, continuity, consistency, and trustworthiness that supports continuous program improvement. This approach involves within and across course alignment, and alignment between courses and clinical experiences. The knowledge distributed across the teacher preparation program in courses or modules and clinical experiences is interconnected, developmentally sequenced, cumulative, and increasingly complex. The instruments used to facilitate course alignment are a course alignment document and an organization structure. The course alignment document supports the interconnectedness among course descriptions, state and national standards, course objectives, course assignments, and the knowledge for teaching (resources). The organizational structure is represented as a sequence of four blocks each containing courses, clinical experiences, state and national standards, and key assessments. Courses in a particular block have interconnected assignments and experiences; and have learning objectives linked to the state and national standards located in the block. Candidates' performance on key assessments indicates their progress towards competent teaching and can indicate strengths and weaknesses in the knowledge base and clinical experiences.

The central ideas regarding clinical experiences in Chapter 6 are guided by a constructivist perspective on learning to teach as represented in the conceptualization of *teaching as an interpretive practice/process*. Clinical experiences involve the application to practice of the knowledge base for teaching and teacher preparation comprised of the best available research, theory, and evidence from practice. The essential practices for learning to teach include the collection of data for planning instruction, the instructional planning process, the enactment of planned instruction, and the assessment of student learning. Particular attention is given to framing the curriculum by positioning new knowledge within the structure of the discipline, focusing on the purpose and benefit of the new knowledge, and contextualizing new knowledge within what students know and value. Guidance for candidates' learning during clinical experiences is focused on essential aspects of competent teaching. Teacher educators and mentor teachers use specific tools to guide learning in clinical experiences including pre-and post-observation instruments and an observation checklist. Clinical experiences occur in authentic contexts with students from diverse cultural and experiential backgrounds.

Chapter 7 presents an approach to monitoring and assessing candidates' progress towards competent teaching through program-embedded key assessments focused on the application of academic knowledge to practice. Key assessments are conducted in the context of coursework and clinical experiences that are interrelated and developmentally sequenced. Candidates' learning in courses and clinical experiences is facilitated by epistemic practices that support the actions, routines, and habits of mind essential for competent teaching. Each key assessment involves observation or participation in an authentic context, documentation that includes evidence and artifacts, analysis and interpretation of data, and a written commentary based on findings from data collection interpreted through the lens of academic knowledge from coursework. The rubric for scoring key assessments consists of four levels, unsatisfactory, basic, proficient, and distinguished. Scoring key assessments is focused on candidates' ability to follow the protocol, adequately analyze and interpret data, and apply findings from data analysis to practice in the written commentary. Each key assessment is scored by at least two individuals, teacher educators or practitioners, who have been trained and calibrated.

Chapter 8 is focused on the interconnectedness of local community and school needs, state and national standards for P-12 education, and teacher preparation. This chapter has three parts that include assessing and responding to local needs, responding to state mandates and standards, and responding to national standards and accreditation requirements. Emphasis is placed on improving P-12 education for the common good and public interest as the overarching purpose for mandates, regulations, and standards imposed on public schools and teacher preparation at the state and national levels. The interconnectedness and singular purpose of state and national mandates provide opportunities for teacher educators to develop responses that simultaneously meet multi-level expectations while focusing on the central purpose of improving P-12 student learning and development through teacher preparation.

Knowledge of the central challenges in the design of teacher preparation informs the work of state and national policy makers. The discussion in this chapter addresses promising practices related to:

- opportunities for candidates to collaborate among peers resulting in communities of practice that support continuous professional development and
- partnership agreements between teacher preparation providers and P-12 schools that include collaborative practice-based research addressing persistent challenges and problems.

Using this Book

This book is primarily written for teacher educators designing and improving teacher preparation programs and for researchers studying practices in programs, and the impact on the performance of program graduates and P-12 student learning outcomes. Additionally, this book will be of interest to graduate students, policymakers, and education practitioners.

This book supports faculty collaboration in designing preservice teacher preparation programs characterized by coherence, continuity, consistency, and trustworthiness. The framework presented in Chapter 3 and elaborated across the subsequent chapters provides guidance for developing the essential characteristics of a trustworthy program. This framework allows for variability across programs based on the context, focus, purpose, and licensure and accreditation requirements. The sequence for program design as represented in the organization of chapters in this book is adaptable. Meeting the conditions for trustworthiness and developing stability in the professional knowledge base for teacher preparation requires that many programs follow the design framework as it is presented. However, when responding to new mandates and requirements, where an established program has all conceptual and structural elements in place, the program explication and course alignment processes can be sequenced and used to make appropriate program adjustments.

The use of state and national standards and licensure requirements in the program explication and course alignment processes in this book is not intended to suggest that the professional knowledge base is limited to such mandates and requirements. These standards and requirements are the minimum for program accreditation, approval, and certification. However, compliance with these standards and requirements does not ensure program trustworthiness in the preparation of candidates with the professional knowledge and skills required for ensuring that all P-12 students meet grade level and subject matter expectations. Developing an adequate knowledge base for program trustworthiness requires that faculty examine the research literature in specific areas related to the knowledge base, examine data on local P-12 student performance, and collect evidence of problems of practice from experienced and novice teachers, other practitioners, and stakeholders.

The program design framework, procedures, and tools presented in this book enable faculty to develop a program that has the integrity and stability necessary for continuous improvement. This framework includes instruments for monitoring candidates' progress toward competent teaching that include key assessments, pre-and post-observation protocols, and an observation checklist. These instruments are linked to the knowledge base represented in coursework. Analysis of data from these instruments can reveal strengths and weaknesses in the knowledge base and practices for developing professional skills. Such an analysis provides evidence for adjustments in programs. Programmatic assessment determines the conceptual and structural integrity of the program.

An academically based teacher preparation program provides many opportunities for productive research that contributes to improving teaching and teacher preparation. The conceptual and structural elements in the design framework presented in this book will help researchers position investigations and generate productive questions. The stability in the program knowledge base, connections among courses, and between courses and clinical experiences will assist researchers in identifying factors contributing to gaps in candidates' knowledge and skills. The availability of assessment instruments used in the program will enable researchers to test their validity and reliability.

This book is especially useful for practitioners when collaborating with teacher educators to design or improve a teacher preparation program. This insider view of the program design process supports practitioners in understanding how to participate in program improvement. Chapter 6 will assist practitioners in understanding how to support candidates during clinical experiences.

Finally, policymakers will find this book useful for developing a deeper understanding of the process of learning to teach, the design of preservice teacher preparation programs, and the research that supports program improvement, candidates' preparation, and learning outcomes for P-12 students. Policy makers can use the understanding gained from this book to advocate for standards that better support improvements in teacher preparation and for increased funding. For example, states are facing teacher shortages in mathematics, science, special education, English learners, career and technical education, and in urban and rural schools. States are developing policies to address teacher shortages and for improving teacher preparation. The success of these efforts is influenced by the effectiveness of state policies and program accreditation practices in addressing three essential issues for improving teacher preparation and learning outcomes for students that include:

- instability in the knowledge base for teaching and teacher preparation,
- disassociation of the knowledge base for teaching from the application to practice in clinical experiences, and
- the use of a cognitive apprenticeship approach to clinical experiences that continuously reproduces existing teaching practices and learning outcomes.

References

Barry, M. N. & Dannenberg, M. (2016). *Out of pocket: The high cost of inadequate high schools and high school student achievement on college affordability*. Washington, DC: Education Reform Now. https://edreformnow.org.

National Council for Accreditation of Teacher Education (NCATE) Blue Ribbon Panel on Clinical Preparation for Improved Student Learning (2010). *Transforming teacher education through clinical practice: A national strategy to prepare effective teachers*. Washington, DC: NCATE.

United States Citizenship and Immigration Services (USCIS) (2018). *2018 USCIS statistical annual report*. Washington, DC: Author.

1

ACADEMICALLY BASED TEACHER PREPARATION

Introduction

The approach presented in this book is for the design of *academically based* preservice teacher preparation. The term academically based preservice teacher preparation is not frequently used; however, the term *academic preparation* is used in referring to the coursework included in university-based teacher preparation programs (Zeichner, 2009). The term *academically taught* is used in the prospectus for Teachers for a New Era (TNE) in describing one of the three design principles for a teacher preparation program:

- A teacher education program should be guided by a respect for evidence.
- Faculty in the arts and sciences disciplines must be fully engaged in the education of prospective teachers.
- Teaching should be recognized as an academically taught clinical-practice profession.

(Kirby, McCombs, Barney, & Naftel, 2006, p. xiv)

The findings from four TNE sites indicate an emphasis on evidence-based practices in teacher preparation involving collaboration among teacher educators, faculty in arts and sciences, and practitioners in partner schools and school districts. Evidence from clinical experiences for candidates and P-12 student learning outcomes in partner schools was used in adjusting university-based course content and assignments (Torrez & Krebs, 2020). This provides insight into the meaning of the term *academically taught clinical-practice profession*.

The discussion in this chapter defines *academically based* teacher preparation, identifies characteristics, and delineates practices. The practices in academically based teacher preparation are illustrated in designing teacher preparation pro-grams, addressing problems of practice, and engaging in continuous improve-ment. The meaning of academically based teacher preparation subsumes the conceptualization of academic coursework and *academically taught clinical practice*.

Defining Academically Based Teacher Preparation

Academically based teacher preparation is a meticulously designed approach grounded in the most reliable research, theory, and practice available; and that employs continuous data gathering and analysis for validation and improvement of practices, outcomes, and impact (Figure 1.1). The conceptual and structural elements within an academically based approach are interconnected and recipro-cal in design and function. The relationship between the philosophical stance (a conceptual element) in a teacher preparation program and candidate recruitment (a structural element) is an example of interconnected and reciprocal design and function. The philosophical stance describes attributes of the candidates recruited for the program, what they will be prepared to do, their target students, the expected outcomes for students, and the impact on communities (Hollins, 2019). The recruitment plan includes a description of the characteristics of potential candidates that match the philosophical stance including knowledge, experiences, dispositions, perceptions, and values; tools for assessing candidates' suitability for the program based on the philosophical stance; and strategies for data gathering

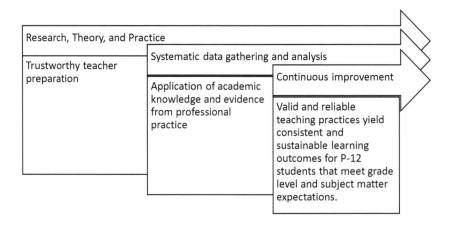

Academically based teacher preparation and teaching engage candidates and teachers in the application of academic knowledge to practice and the continuous observation and documentation of studentsttj responses for the purpose of improving teaching practices and learning outcomes.

FIGURE 1.1 Academically based teacher preparation and teaching

for validation and improvement. *Academically based* preservice teacher preparation is supported by purposefully designed clinical experiences located in authentic settings and focused on the preparation for teaching students from diverse cultural and experiential backgrounds and with different needs.

Embedded within an academically based approach to teacher preparation is an approach to academically based teaching practices. Academically based teaching practices are grounded in theory, research, evidence from practice, and continuous improvement of learning outcomes through the process of observation, documentation, and analysis. Clinical experiences provide candidates opportunities for developing the habits of mind and practices associated with academically based teaching. Academically based teaching practices are modeled in the program design, and in pedagogies and learning experiences provided for candidates. Facilitating candidates' learning during clinical experiences is an example of modeling academic teaching practices. During clinical experiences, candidates learn to make observations, document teaching practices and students' responses, and to use knowledge of students, subject matter, and pedagogy in planning learning experiences. Candidates learn to use academic tools such as a class profile, curriculum mapping, curriculum framing, learning cycle, and teaching cycle to enhance instructional planning and to develop more powerful learning experiences. Candidates learn to rely on research, theory, and documented evidence from their own practice to increase their understanding of teaching and learning.

Academically based teaching practices are guided by knowledge of learners and learning, including that on child and adolescent growth and development, a theoretical perspective and discipline specific research. The conceptualization of academically based teaching practices employed in subsequent chapters in this book is referred to as *teaching as an interpretive practice/process*. Teaching as an interpretive practice/process is based on a constructivist theoretical perspective. This approach incorporates a teaching cycle of planning based on knowledge of students, subject matter, and pedagogy; enactment of planned learning experiences; observation and documentation of students' responses during the planned learning experiences; and interpretation and translation of students' responses to learning experiences for evidence to inform subsequent planning (Hollins, 2011). Teaching as an interpretive practice/process is supported during clinical experiences using specifically designed instruments including the pre-observation conference format, observation checklist, and post observation conference described in Chapter 6; and key assessments described in Chapter 7. Incorporated within each of these instruments are the habits of mind, and professional knowledge and practices associated with academically based teaching, specifically teaching as an interpretive practice.

Identifying Characteristics of Academically Based Teacher Preparation Programs

Academically based teacher preparation programs include central and instrumental characteristics. Central characteristics include coherence, continuity, consistency,

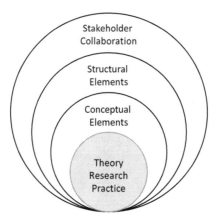

Academically based teacher preparation is grounded in knowledge from theory, research, and practice; organized around conceptual and structural elements; and developed and maintained through provider and stakeholder collaboration and participation.

FIGURE 1.2 Academically based teacher preparation program design

and trustworthiness. Instrumental characteristics include collaboration, interrelatedness of conceptual and structural elements, and systematic data collection. The central characteristics are program quality indicators. Instrumental characteristics are essential for program development, continuous improvement, and meeting the expectations of the quality indicators.

Central Characteristics

The central characteristics of academically based teacher preparation guide program design. For example, coherence is developed through the methodical alignment of professional knowledge within and across courses, and with application to practice in clinical experiences (Canrinus, Klette, & Hammerness, 2019; DeLuca & Bellara, 2013). In the process of learning to teach, professional knowledge is aligned and applied when examining and planning student learning experiences. Specific aspects of methodically aligned professional knowledge are applied during clinical experiences in the observation, documentation, and analysis of teaching, learning, and the social context in classrooms. In planning instruction, professional knowledge is applied in framing the curriculum and creating learning experiences.

Continuity is the developmental sequencing of methodically aligned professional knowledge and clinical experiences to foster learning that is interrelated, increasingly complex, and cumulative (Zeichner, 2009). This developmental sequencing provides opportunities for positioning benchmarks for assessing candidates' progress in developing the knowledge and skills required for competent teaching, providing interventions when necessary, and evaluating the effectiveness of aspects of the teacher preparation program.

Consistency refers to stability of professional knowledge and clinical experiences over time. The professional knowledge base and clinical experiences are based on the best research, theory, and practice available at the time of program design or redesign. The opportunity for developing coherence and continuity in a teacher preparation program depends on stability in professional knowledge and clinical experiences. Maintaining coherence and continuity in a program requires purposeful adjustments and interventions for improvement.

There are three recognized sources for changes in the professional knowledge base and clinical experiences. First, changes are in response to new knowledge derived from valid and reliable research, theory, and practice in the field. Second, changes are in response to the analysis of data collected in the program or at the clinical experience site. Third, changes are in response to state or national mandates for teacher preparation, requirements for accreditation, or mandated changes in the P-12 school curriculum or school practices. The proposed changes are carefully examined and aligned within the existing professional knowledge base and clinical experiences, rather than unnecessarily expanding the knowledge base to include new content or experiences. This can result in adjustments in the content and framing of the existing professional knowledge base and clinical experiences.

Trustworthiness is based on the quality and consistency in the preparation of candidates, their performance as teachers in the classroom, and learning and developmental outcomes for their students. The combination of coherence, continuity, and consistency form the foundation for trustworthiness. When any one of the other central characteristics is absent, trustworthiness is compromised. Data collected on programs that do not meet the conditions of the quality indicators are unlikely to provide reliable evidence for substantive improvements, except in identifying the absence of these characteristics. In the absence of program quality indicators, program graduates often depend on knowledge gained from mentors during clinical experiences and colleagues in schools where they are placed as full-time teachers. Some teachers from these programs will develop high levels of competence, others will remain low-performing teachers for the duration of their careers. Programs with such unreliable and inconsistent outcomes are not trustworthy.

Instrumental Characteristics

The central characteristics for academically based teacher preparation are supported by three instrumental characteristics that include:

1. collaboration among faculty participants and contributors, school partners and other stakeholders;
2. interrelatedness of conceptual and structural elements in the program; and

3. systematic data collection, analysis, and the application of findings for the improvement of program practices.

These instrumental characteristics provide the context and process for developing the central characteristics of academically based teacher preparation.

Collaboration

Collaboration among faculty participants and contributors, partners, and other stakeholders is essential for determining the appropriateness, relevance, and interconnectedness among professional knowledge, clinical experiences, the P-12 school curriculum, and the school context (Burroughs, et. al., 2020). Teacher education faculty collaborate in identifying the most valid and reliable research, theory, and practice available to form the professional knowledge base for learning to teach. Further, the teacher education faculty is responsible for ensuring that the program meets the expectations for academically based teacher preparation and the mandates and standards for state and national accreditation. Teacher education faculty collaborate with practitioners in partner schools to identify problems of practice, changes in school conditions, and new mandates that influence or require adjustments in professional knowledge and skills (Ball, 2000). Teacher education faculty and school partners collaborate in designing and sequencing clinical experiences.

Faculty in the arts and sciences are responsible for the specific subject matter preparation of teacher candidates. Teacher education faculty are responsible for ensuring that the subject matter preparation of teacher candidates meets the required state and national standards for program accreditation, candidate knowledge assessments, and the requirements for the specific curriculum expectations for elementary, middle, and secondary school students. The responsibilities shared by teacher education faculty and faculty in the arts and sciences require collaboration to ensure that candidates meet expectations for professional knowledge and specific subject matter knowledge for teaching (Ball, Thames, & Phelps, 2008).

Interrelatedness of Conceptual and Structural Elements

The conceptual and structural elements form the foundational context for the central characteristics of academically based teacher preparation. The interrelatedness of these elements is at the core of program coherence. The conceptual elements include the philosophical stance, theoretical perspective, professional knowledge and skills, and epistemic practices. Systematic correlation exists within and between conceptual and structural elements in the teacher preparation program. For example, the interrelationship between the philosophical stance and the theoretical perspective frames the professional knowledge and skills in the teacher preparation program. Epistemic practices embody and model the application of the philosophical stance and theoretical perspective while engaging candidates in learning experiences that develop the professional knowledge, skills, and habits of mind associated with competent teaching (see Chapter 3). An example of the interrelatedness of the conceptual and structural elements is the correlation of admission practices with the philosophical stance. The philosophical stance describes the target population to be prepared in the teacher preparation program, what candidates will be prepared to do, and the target student population to be served. Admission practices identify, select, and admit candidates with the appropriate characteristics and potential for success in the program and in the profession.

Any weakness in the interrelatedness within and between the conceptual and structural elements is a threat to the integrity of the central characteristics in an academically based teacher preparation program. For example, seemingly minor isolated idiosyncratic changes in the professional knowledge base made by an individual faculty can cause a ripple effect that disrupts each of the central characteristics (coherence, continuity, consistency, and trustworthiness) within and across conceptual and structural elements. Even slight changes in the professional knowledge base (conceptual element) can impact candidates' performance on the related formative and summative assessments (structural element).

Systematic Data Collection

A primary purpose for data collection in an academically based teacher preparation program is to validate and maintain the central and instrumental characteristics and determine the extent to which the expected outcomes are achieved. Through the process of data collection and analysis, weaknesses in the program are identified and ameliorated. Data collection, analysis, and the application of findings in improving practices is essential for maintaining the central characteristics.

Determining and maintaining the trustworthiness of a teacher preparation program requires multiple data sources and multiple measures for the conceptual and structural elements. For example, evidence for the conceptual element of professional knowledge can be provided by compiling a table of publications including the research, theory, and practice linked to developmentally sequenced courses or modules and specific clinical experiences provided for candidates in the program. This table of professional knowledge provides evidence for the structural element addressing the alignment of courses and clinical experiences. Tracking changes in professional knowledge and making comparisons with candidates' application of professional knowledge to practice using monitoring instruments such as key assessments and the teaching observation checklist (see Chapter 6) are indicators for the integrity of the professional knowledge and learning experiences provided for candidates.

Instruments used to collect data for monitoring candidates' progress in learning to teach often differ from those used for assessing readiness for teaching and teaching competence (Caughlan & Jiang, 2014). Monitoring progress is focused on candidates' understanding and application of specific professional knowledge to practice and developing the habits of mind associated with competent teaching. Teaching evaluation is focused on pedagogical practices, classroom environment, and students' developmental outcomes. The EdTPA is an example of a teaching performance assessment for measuring readiness for teaching that is used in many states as one factor in determining qualification for teacher licensure (Sato, 2014). The Network for Educator Effectiveness is a comprehensive, research-based framework for inservice teaching evaluation and professional development sponsored by the University of Missouri (https://neeadvantage.com). Framework for Teaching: Evaluation Instrument (Danielson, 2013) and Classroom Assessment Scoring System (CLASS) (LaParo, Pianta, & Stuhlman, 2004) are used to measure teaching competence for both preservice teachers and inservice teachers. Many states have mandated evaluation systems such as the Missouri's Educator Evaluation System (2013). Other states have developed standards that inform teaching evaluation such as the California Standards for the Teaching Profession (2009). Each of these approaches and instruments provide useful data for informing improvements in teacher preparation program practices (Gitomer & Zisk, 2015).

State and national accreditation agencies set teacher preparation program standards and standards for data collection. For example, the Council for the Accreditation of Educator Preparation (CAEP) has five standards and eight annual reporting measures. Similarly, the Association for Advancing Quality Educator Preparation (AAQEP) has four standards and ten sections to its required annual report. Two common factors addressed by both national accrediting agencies include performance indicators and continuous growth and improvement. An important difference between the two organizations is that CAEP is recognized by the Council for High Education Accreditation (CHEA) and AAQEP is not. The rigorous standards held by CAEP in compliance with CHEA result in consequential decisions that can negatively affect accreditation status such as denial, probation, and revocation. Rigorous and consequential standards are important for the advancement of the profession in all areas, including the preparation of teachers for diversity and P-12 student academic performance.

Facilitating Learning in Academically Based Teacher Preparation

In academically based teacher preparation, all learning experiences are purposefully developed, developmentally sequenced, interrelated, and framed by the philosophical stance and theoretical perspective. Learning experiences provide candidates with frequent opportunities for observation, documentation, and application of professional knowledge to practice in schools and classrooms.

Epistemic pedagogies and protocols support the development of deep knowledge and habits of mind characteristic of competent teaching.

Early clinical experiences are methodically guided to support candidates in developing the habits of mind and practices characteristic of competent teaching. Candidates engage in observation, documentation, and analysis of teaching practices, student learning experiences, and students' responses to learning experiences by applying professional knowledge gained through academic study of research, theory, and practice. Specific protocols and tools are used to support candidates' learning and to provide consistency and continuity. Advanced clinical experiences provide opportunities for candidates to learn from more fully engaging in teaching under the careful supervision of experienced teachers and teacher educators. Candidates develop detailed instructional plans that reveal the extent of their understanding and ability to apply professional knowledge to practice (see Chapter 6). Examples of evidence supporting detailed instructional planning include a community profile, class profile, individual student development inventories, curriculum map, and the curriculum framing process. Mentor teachers and teacher educators have a shared understanding of the practices and protocols used to facilitate, monitor, and assess candidates learning during advanced clinical practice. Examples of protocols for clinical supervision include pre- and post-observation conference formats and an observation instrument or rubric.

Designing Academically Based Teacher Preparation

Academically based teacher preparation programs have specific characteristics; however, there are often wide variations in purpose, theoretical perspectives, the framing of professional knowledge, and epistemic pedagogies that support candidate learning. Similarly, there are wide variations in the corresponding structural elements that support the conceptual elements for the program, including program admission practices, alignment of courses and clinical experiences, school partnerships, assessment of professional knowledge and skills, and programmatic assessment. These variations among academically based teacher preparation programs are based on local needs and collaboration among local stakeholders and providers. Further, how programs are positioned or situated based on providers and sponsors influence variation. Examples of program sponsors include colleges, universities, school districts, foundations, and other community-based organizations. However, maintaining high quality professional preparation requires that all teacher preparation programs meet specific expectations for preparation and completer performance, and that there is a common assessment for licensure based on grade level and subject area. This requirement is to ensure the quality of education provided for students in the nation's public schools.

The discussion in this book presents an approach used in designing a university based preservice teacher preparation program. The conceptual and structural elements are very similar for academically based teacher preparation programs regardless of location. For example, all academically based programs include professional knowledge based on research, theory, and practice. However, the framing and delivery structure for professional knowledge might differ. The framing of professional knowledge is related to the purpose, local context, and local needs. Professional knowledge for programs designed to prepare teachers for urban schools might place more emphasis on the role of culture and experience in child and adolescent growth and development, and the role of the home language in teaching early literacy than in programs with a different focus. There are multiple delivery structures for professional knowledge including courses, modules, independent study, online and in-person group study. There are variations in arrangements for clinical experiences including course related practicums, student teaching, internships, and residencies. There are variations in monitoring, guidance, supervision, and assessment. The approach presented in this book can be adjusted to accommodate most situations in designing or improving an academically based preservice teacher preparation program.

Developing an effective academically based preservice teacher preparation program requires collaboration among providers and stakeholders. The providers are those responsible for administering the program and recommending candidates for licensure. The stakeholders are those who contribute knowledge that is academic, practice, or service based; cultural and community knowledge; schools and other employers of program graduates; local agencies and businesses; and others who benefit or have interest in public education. This is not an exhaustive list of potential collaborators. Circumstances and situations can reveal the need for stakeholders not previously included in such collaboration. The recent coronavirus pandemic has increased awareness of the need for teacher educators and school practitioners to collaborate with health care providers regarding the developmental and medical needs of children and adolescents. The collaboration among teacher preparation providers and stakeholders is focused on specific aspects of teacher preparation related to the expertise, benefit, contribution, and interests of the participants. Often, collaboration is focused on local needs, problems of practice, professional knowledge and skills, clinical experiences, and requirements for state and national accreditation.

Designing a new academically based preservice teacher preparation program requires synthesizing, organizing, and applying knowledge from multiple sources including collaboration with stakeholders, research, theory, and evidence from practice. Synthesizing information from multiple sources requires identifying connections among ideas, grouping related ideas, and creating labels that form categories. Information organized into categories can be applied as the initial basis for courses or modules of professional knowledge for teaching and teacher preparation. Additional sources for professional knowledge include the professional associations (e.g., International literacy Association, National Council of Teachers of Mathematics, etc.), InTASC Model Core Teaching Standards and Learning

Progressions (2013), the National Board for Professional Teaching Standards (www.nbpts.org), the Council for the Accreditation of Educator Preparation (www.caepnet.org), and state standards for accreditation. The alignment and developmental sequencing of professional knowledge across courses or modules requires collaboration among developers. The alignment of modules of professional knowledge with clinical experiences requires collaboration among program providers and practitioners.

Clinical experiences that provide opportunities for observation, documentation, analysis, and application of academic knowledge to practice are an essential feature of academically based teacher preparation. Clinical experiences are guided by those with deep academic knowledge of schools, students, and teaching practices in collaboration with colleagues who have deep knowledge and expertise in the daily practices in schools, classroom teaching, and the local community. Academics and practitioners collaborate in developing shared understanding and practices for guiding candidates' progress in the application of professional knowledge to practice. Common protocols and instruments are used. The guidance of candidates during clinical experiences is more fully discussed in Chapter 6.

Addressing Problems of Practice

The range of problems of practice related to the design and implementation of preservice teacher preparation programs addressed in the scholarly literature is broad and complex. However, the problems of practice addressed in this book are limited to those that directly impact the design of preservice teacher preparation programs. The problems addressed include those directly related to developing professional knowledge, learning to apply professional knowledge to practice, and developing appropriate subject matter knowledge.

Developing Professional Knowledge

A pivotal problem of practice in university based preservice teacher preparation is individual faculty ownership of courses and programs. In many instances, faculty develop courses in isolation, and change content and experiences based on personal preferences. At times, faculty serving as program coordinators change the sequence of courses, eliminate, or replace courses based on personal discretion and without consultation with colleagues or stakeholders. These situations contribute to instability in the professional knowledge base in preservice programs; and leave faculty who are responsible for recommending candidates for licensure unable to warrant the professional knowledge or readiness of program graduates for classroom teaching. The national policy response to this situation has been more restrictive state and national standards and increased standardized testing to determine competence. Such policy responses do not guarantee that learning outcomes will improve for P-12 students.

Improving learning outcomes for P-12 students requires changes in the design of preservice teacher preparation that stabilize the professional knowledge base. This means collaboration among those developing modules for professional knowledge and learning experiences, agreement on how and what knowledge to use from multiple sources, and how knowledge is to be framed based on the philosophical stance. Monitoring and assessing candidates' understanding and application of professional knowledge and its impact on P-12 learning validate the professional knowledge base and reveal areas for improvement.

Applying Professional Knowledge to Practice

Problems related to the application of professional knowledge to practice in preservice teacher preparation are from multiple sources including instability in professional knowledge, misalignment of professional knowledge and clinical experiences, mismatch between professional knowledge for candidates and teaching practices in classrooms, and differences in feedback candidates receive from teacher mentors in schools and academic supervisors (Zeichner, 2009).

Instability in professional knowledge can be confusing to candidates and mentor teachers. Often candidates assigned to the same module of professional knowledge taught by different instructors, receive different content and assignments. This diminishes the valuable collaboration among candidates that fosters deep understanding of different approaches in the application of professional knowledge and its impact on P-12 students' learning and development. Instability in the professional knowledge base contributes to uncertainty and confusion for mentor teachers regarding the focus of guidance and feedback provided for candidates. The mutual and reciprocal benefit of clinical experiences for candidates and mentor teachers is compromised.

The misalignment of professional knowledge and clinical experiences occurs in the absence of careful collaborative planning and methodical program design. Assignments and learning experiences that link professional knowledge and clinical experiences are essential for program alignment that supports mutual and reciprocal learning among candidates, mentor teachers, and academic supervisors (Zeichner, 2009).

This collaborative approach to clinical experiences is especially important for the continuous improvement of teaching practices and learning outcomes for students. A persistent challenge in teacher preparation expressed by university faculty is the mismatch between teaching practices in schools and the professional knowledge candidates learn in courses. The collaboration between providers and practitioners has a mutual and reciprocal benefit. Providers maintain contact with the realities of classroom teaching, the opportunities, and impediments in the application of professional knowledge to practice. Practitioners learn about new knowledge in the field, analyze and improve their own practices through collaborating with providers and providing guidance for candidates.

Developing Appropriate Subject Matter Knowledge

Subject matter for teaching goes beyond the usual content required for an academic major. Shulman (1990) pointed out that:

> The abstractness of a disciplinary subject is convenient for the purposes of its own study, which is what the scholar in the university does. However, professional practitioners must see concrete connections of subject matter and method with the rest of the world of knowledge and culture and with the life of real people in society.
>
> *(p. 304)*

Subject matter knowledge for teaching has specific characteristics (Ball et al., 2008). First, subject matter knowledge for teaching requires alignment with the school curriculum at the level for which the candidate will be licensed. The alignment of subject matter knowledge for teaching includes and extends beyond knowledge in the school curriculum to enable teachers to frame the curriculum and develop appropriate learning experiences for specific groups of students. For example, the school curriculum for teaching early literacy may not include materials and experiences related to children from diverse, cultural, linguistic, and experiential backgrounds; however, framing the curriculum and developing effective learning experiences requires knowledge beyond the school curriculum. Similarly, the school curriculum in secondary English may not address ethnic minority literature; however, knowledge of this literature is essential for framing the curriculum and developing meaningful and productive learning experiences for ethnic minority students.

Second, subject matter knowledge for teaching requires knowledge of the structure of the discipline and disciplinary practices. Teaching requires knowledge of the big ideas, principles, concepts, relationships among concepts, and the application of big ideas, principles, and concepts to practice in a discipline. This knowledge forms the basis for understanding and developing learning progressions, supporting students in developing functional cognitive schemas, and correcting conceptual misunderstandings. Knowledge of disciplinary practices includes understanding methods of inquiry, the development and validation of new knowledge, and how new knowledge is represented and presented within the discipline and to the public. These disciplinary practices form the basis for developing learning experiences.

Third, subject matter knowledge for teaching requires understanding the application of knowledge to practice in everyday life and in occupations and professions. Understanding subject matter knowledge in this way amplifies purpose and meaning in teaching and learning. Providing students opportunities for applying knowledge to practice in their everyday lives and observing its application to practice in occupations and professions increases value and depth of understanding.

The different ways of knowing subject matter essential for teaching are developed from discipline specific courses taught in arts and sciences and methods of teaching learned in preservice teacher preparation programs. Ensuring that candidates develop the subject matter knowledge essential for teaching requires collaboration among faculty in arts and sciences and teacher educators whether located at a college, university, or elsewhere.

Engaging Continuous Improvement

Continuous improvement is a process of purposeful data gathering, analysis, and application to practice for advancing the effectiveness of preservice teacher preparation and knowledge of teaching and learning to teach. The central focus of continuous improvement in an academically based preservice teacher preparation program is to determine the extent to which the qualities of coherence, continuity, consistency, and trustworthiness are maintained. These qualities are reflected in data collected on the conceptual and structural elements of the program and can reveal strengths, weaknesses, inconsistencies, and outcomes.

Data collection on one aspect of the conceptual elements can provide information on other conceptual elements as well as on specific structural elements. For example, data collected on candidates' application of academic knowledge to practice can provide information on coherence, continuity, and consistency in the presentation of academic knowledge (conceptual) and on the availability of opportunities in clinical experiences for application to practice (structural). Further, these data can provide

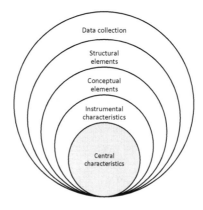

Continuous improvement is the process of monitoring, assessing, and increasing program effectiveness through data collection and analysis on the central and instrumental characteristics evident in conceptual and structural elements to determine appropriateness for achieving expectations, outcomes, and impact.

FIGURE 1.3 Continuous improvement

information about the appropriateness and relevance of academic knowledge in the application to practice. These data provide information useful for adjustments in academic knowledge and clinical experiences.

Conclusion

The discussion in this chapter has presented academically based teacher preparation as grounded in research, theory, and evidence from practice. The quality indicators of academically based teacher preparation are coherence, continuity, consistency, and trustworthiness. These quality indicators are the central characteristics. The instrumental characteristics are collaboration among stakeholders, interrelatedness among conceptual and structural elements, and systematic data collection. These factors foster the stability in program practices that is essential for reliable data collection and productive interventions that support continuous improvement and the development of trustworthiness. Collaboration among stakeholders is essential for data analysis and interpretation, and the development and implementation of productive interventions.

References

Ball, D. L. (2000). Bridging practices: Intertwining content and pedagogy in teaching and learning to teach. *Journal of Teacher Education*, 51 (3), 241–247.

Ball, D. L., Thames, M. H., & Phelps, G. (2008). Content knowledge for teaching: What makes it special. *Journal of Teacher Education*, 59 (5), 389–407.

Burroughs, G., Lewis, A., Battey, D., Curran, M., Hyland, N. E., & Rya, S. (2020). From mediated fieldwork to co-constructed partnerships: A Framework for guiding and reflecting on P-12 school-university partnerships. *Journal of Teacher Education*, 71 (1), 122–134.

California Standards for the Teaching Profession (2009). www.ctc.ca.gov/docs/default-source/educator-prep/standards/cstp-2009.pdf.

Canrinus, E. T., Klette, K., & Hammerness, K. (2019). Diversity in coherence: Strengths and opportunities of three programs. *Journal of Teacher Education*, 70 (3), 192–205.

Caughlan, S. & Jiang, H. (2014). Observation and teacher quality: Critical analysis of observational instruments in preservice teacher performance assessment. *Journal of Teacher Education*, 65 (5), 375–388.

Council of Chief State School Officers (2013*). InTASC model core teaching standards and learning progressions*. Washington, DC: Author. www.ccsso.org/intasc.

Danielson, C. (2013). *The framework for teaching: Evaluation instrument*. Chicago: Danielson Group Publishers.

DeLuca, C. & Bellara, A. (2013). The current state of assessment education: Aligning policy, standards, and teacher education curriculum. *Journal of Teacher Education*, 64 (4), 356–372.

Gitomer, D. H. & Zisk, R. C. (2015). Knowing what teachers know. *Review of Research in Education*, 39, 1–53.

Hollins, E. R. (2019). *Teaching to transform urban schools and communities: Powerful pedagogy in practice*. New York: Routledge.

Kirby, S. N., McCombs, J. S., Barney, H., & Naftel, S. (2006). Implementation progress and thoughts about sustainability of TNE. In S. N. Kirby, J. S. McCombs, H. Barney, & S. Naftel, *Reforming teacher education: Something old and something new* (pp. 69–84). Santa Monica, CA: Rand Corporation.

LaParo, K. M., Pianta, R. C., & Stuhlman, M. (2004). The classroom assessment scoring system: Findings from the prekindergarten year. *The Elementary School Journal*, 104 (5), 409–426.

Missouri's Educator Evaluation System (n.d.). *Teacher evaluation*. www.nctq.org/dmsView/01-TeacherEvaluationProtocol.

Sato, M. (2014). What is the underlying conception of teaching of the edTPA? *Journal of Teacher Education*, 65 (5), 421–434.

Shulman, L. S. (1990). Reconnecting the foundations to the substance of teacher education. *Teachers College Record*, 91 (3), 300–310.

Torrez, C. A. & Krebs, M. (2020). *The teacher residency model: Core components for high impact on student achievement*. Lanham, MD: The Rowan & Littlefield Publishing Group, Inc.

Zeichner, K. (2009). Rethinking the connections between campus courses and field experiences in college- and university-based teacher education. *Journal of Teacher Education*, December 30. https://doi.org/10.1177/0022487109347671.

2

COLLABORATION AMONG TEACHER EDUCATORS AND WITH STAKEHOLDERS

Introduction

Faculty collaboration is essential for interpreting and translating to practice research and theory in teaching and teacher preparation, and for responding to state and national standards. Collaboration among faculty involves teamwork leading to a community of practice that promotes collective ownership of programs, consensus on the professional knowledge base for competent teaching, and core and epistemic practices that guide learning to teach. A community of practice engages in continuous improvement of teacher preparation based on evidence from candidates' performance on formative and summative assessments and the impact on P-12 student learning, growth, and development. Collaboration in a community of practice is essential for academically based teacher preparation programs to ensure that:

- the quality indicators of coherence, continuity, and consistency are met;
- professional knowledge is comprehensive, cumulative, and increasingly complex;
- courses and clinical experiences are interrelated and developmentally sequenced; and
- knowledge from courses is observed, analyzed, and applied in clinical experiences.

Developing a teacher preparation program with these characteristics requires purposeful collaboration among teacher educators and between teacher educators, faculty from other disciplines, practitioners in the field and other stakeholders.

Context for Program Development

Many university and schools of education policies regarding tenure and promotion encourage individualistic, idiosyncratic, and competitive accomplishments in scholarship, teaching, and service. At research intensive institutions, developing a reputation in the field is often more important than contributing to a high-quality preservice teacher preparation program. It is difficult to reconcile such priorities with the evidence that teachers influence the quality of life for individuals, families, and communities. However, such values and priorities are evident in the resources allocated to preservice teacher preparation programs, including the number of full-time faculty versus adjuncts, the assignment of faculty load (courses and supervising clinical experiences), and the evaluation of teacher educators' accomplishments (Beck & Kosnik, 2002; Ginsberg & Rhodes, 2003). These values and priorities limit the time available for engaging in collaborative teamwork, developing communities of practice, and continuous program improvement as required for achieving excellence in candidate preparation and for national accreditation.

Wilkins, Young, and Sterner (2009) conducted a study of 80 teacher preparation programs in universities accredited by the National Council for the Accreditation of Teacher Education (NCATE). The study focused on NCATE's Standard 2, Element 3 (Assessment System and Unit Evaluation: Use of Data for Program Improvement). These researchers reported that teacher preparation programs were "creating and implementing assessment systems to measure candidate performance, aligning program design and delivery with those assessments, and making use of aggregated data to make informed improvements" (p. 14). The findings from this study were that the most common areas of program improvement were changes in curriculum, assessment systems, unit and program structures, and admission and advising practices. Often, existing courses were redesigned, and new courses were developed. The time in clinical experiences was lengthened and structures were changed.

Trend data from the National Center for Education Statistics (NCES, 2013) shows that changes in teacher preparation programs in response to 50 years of NCATE standards and accreditation requirements may have had a limited positive impact on student learning outcomes. The NCES trend data reveal that from 1971–2012, 9-year-olds gained 13 points in reading, 13-year-olds gained eight points, and 17-year-olds gained two points. The NCES trend data reveal that from 1973–2012, in mathematics, 9-year-olds gained 25 points, 12-year-olds gained 19 points, and 17-year-olds gained two points. However, the nation's report card (NCES, 2019) shows that 41% of fourth graders, 34% of eighth graders, and 25% of twelfth graders scored at proficient or above in mathematics. In reading (NCES, 2019), 35% of fourth graders, 34% of eighth graders, and 37% of twelfth graders scored at proficient or above. These student scores and levels of proficiency raise questions about teaching practices and teacher preparation that are not adequately addressed in the program changes found in the study conducted by Wilkins, Young, and Sterner (2009). Faculty collaborative inquiry into the knowledge base and experiences for learning to teach is essential for making productive changes that improve candidates' learning and learning outcomes for P-12 students.

For example, Wolsey, Young, Scales et al., (2013) conducted a study of candidate perception of literacy practices learned in their teacher preparation program as compared to the signature features of the program and faculty intent. Program content in literacy and candidates' perceptions were contextualized within the 2003–2010 Standards for the Teaching Profession of the International Reading Association. The study included elementary teacher preparation programs across ten different universities. These researchers found that theory into practice, balanced literacy, and assessment to inform instruction were common signature features across all programs. Faculty and candidates agreed on the signature features of their program, and that diversity was an area that needed improvement. Candidates felt confident in their knowledge of curriculum and instruction, and somewhat confident in using assessment to inform instruction. Candidates felt less confident in how and when to apply their knowledge in some areas of literacy. In essence, candidates were confident in declarative knowledge, but less confident in procedural and conditional knowledge.

These studies by Wilkins, Young, and Sterner (2009) and Wolsey, Young, Scales et al., (2013) reveal the need for deeper analysis of data collected in compliance with standards for the profession and for national accreditation. Comparing program focus and faculty intent with outcomes and candidate perceptions is especially important in interpreting and translating findings from data collection to practice. In addition to meeting national standards for data collection, collaborative teamwork among faculty in preservice teacher preparation is necessary for examining and rethinking existing program practices for the purpose of:

- Determining the professional knowledge base and developmental sequencing that support progress towards competent teaching and that addresses problems of practice in the field;
- Identifying approaches to clinical experiences that go beyond the traditional apprenticeship model in providing opportunities for developing deep insights and professional skills through focused inquiry, directed observation, and guided practice in the application of knowledge from coursework;
- Incorporating epistemic practices into preservice coursework, clinical experiences, and assessments that promote the habits of mind and practices that support developing and implementing meaningful and productive experiences for the learning and development of children and youth; and
- Developing a trustworthy approach to monitoring candidates' progress towards competent teaching in the preservice teacher preparation program over time.

These factors are at the core of program design, evaluation, and continuous improvement.

Leadership for Collaborative Teamwork

Leadership for collaborative teamwork and for a community of practice among faculty in preservice teacher preparation requires a theoretically grounded approach. In this case, a holistic transformative approach was employed (Shields, 2011). This approach requires that leaders have a clear vision for competent teaching as the outcome for well-designed and high-quality teacher preparation, the outcomes of schooling, the impact of individual teachers on school practices, and the impact of schooling on individuals and communities. This vision informs leadership; but is not a mandate for designing preservice teacher preparation. Holistic transformative leaders are knowledgeable and responsive to the cultural, social, and political context in which teacher preparation programs are located. They understand and respect the expertise and divergent values and views among faculty and support opportunities for expression, negotiation, and consensus. Holistic transformative leaders facilitate faculty dialogue in collectively examining state and national standards, standards set by professional organizations, the scholarly literature, and problems of practice. In their discussions, faculty collaboratively identify and agree upon approaches for addressing program design and tasks to be completed. The tools and support necessary for accomplishing tasks associated with developing a well-designed and high-quality teacher preparation program are provided.

The approach used in the case example presented in this discussion involved a collaborative leadership team. The formation of the leadership team began with the appointment of a facilitator for program renewal. In July 2015, the interim dean invited the endowed chair for urban teacher education to facilitate the teacher preparation program renewal. The facilitator was expected to work collaboratively with the division chair. The endowed chair was familiar with the scholarly literature on teacher preparation, served on the council for the national accreditation agency, had previous experience designing and redesigning teacher preparation programs at several other universities, and had expertise in diversity, secondary social studies education, and elementary literacy development. The division chair had detailed knowledge of the institutional practices and procedures for course and program approval, systems for data collection, and timelines; detailed knowledge of programs and experience in program leadership; and expertise in elementary mathematics education and music education. The coordinator for secondary English was added as the third member of the leadership team. The third member of the leadership team was a junior faculty with extensive knowledge of the scholarly literature on teacher preparation, special interest in the impact of state policies on the preparation of teachers, and expertise in secondary English and history education.

The roles and responsibilities of each member of the leadership team were clearly delineated. The facilitator for program renewal, in collaboration with the other two leadership team members, was responsible for developing the vision

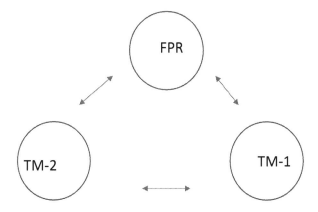

The leadership team met bi-weekly. The facilitator for program renewal (FPR) met separately with each team member as necessary. The two team members met as necessary.

FIGURE 2.1 Leadership team collaboration

and approach for the collaborative teamwork, planning and facilitating meetings of the teacher preparation faculty and other stakeholders, monitoring progress, and meeting timelines. The division chair was responsible for compiling data and documents related to the existing status of credential programs and clinical experiences, preparing course and program documents for the university approval process, making corrections to the website for teacher licensure areas, updating and revising handbooks and other program manuals, and monitoring the progress of programs through the state approval process. The third member of the leadership team communicated directly with the state department of education and kept the team and faculty apprised of expectations and changes, worked collaboratively with the division chair on the preparation of data and documents required for state program approval, assisted with the development of tools and protocols for supporting collaborative teamwork, and developed worked examples using new tools and protocols.

Collaboration among Teacher Educators

Teacher educators frequently collaborate on research projects, co-author books and manuscripts for publication in professional journals; however, the type of collaboration that results in programs characterized by coherence, continuity, and consistency is much more challenging. Historically, teacher preparation programs have consisted of loosely related courses and clinical experiences where faculty developed courses in isolation and individuals assumed ownership and exercised academic freedom in course development. In this situation, two sections of the same course taught by different instructors can have different content and learning experiences. This type of fluidity in course content and learning experiences makes it difficult to know what candidates learn in the program and for educator preparation providers to assume responsibility for the performance of program completers.

The challenges of faculty collaboration in higher education were the subject of two seminal studies (Quinlan & Akerlind, 2000; Briggs, 2007). Quinlan and Akerlind (2000) conducted a study of two cases of "department-based, practice-centered peer inquiry projects" (p. 23). One project was in a history department at a state university and the other was an engineering department at a reputable private university. The history department project consisted of a series of "teaching circles" based on faculty generated topics of interest. The teaching circles provided opportunities for faculty to discuss issues and problems related to teaching and learning. Attendance at the teaching circles was voluntary and varied with each topic. The leaders for the engineering project developed an approach to discussing teaching, learning, and pedagogy for the purpose of improving the assessment of faculty teaching performance and faculty incentives. The approach involved six faculty meeting six times for two hours over the academic year to identify the elements of "good teaching," to video tape and critique segments of teaching in their courses.

Quinlan and Akerlind (2000) found that "in both departments, faculty appreciation and understanding of their colleagues' perspectives seemed to increase as a consequence of the project" (p. 43). Further, the researchers pointed out that "the collaborative interactions were an opportunity to bridge the subcultures within the departments, creating an occasion for dialogue and increased understanding and respect among differing factions" (p. 43). These collaborative teaching projects did not appear to change the fundamental pedagogical beliefs of the participating faculty, and teaching practices were altered in only a few instances.

Briggs (2007) investigated how departments engage in collaboration for continuous program planning for improvement in undergraduate general education. Briggs (2007) pointed out that "regardless of their source, calls for institutional accountability and curricular coherence suggest that faculty must collaborate more than they have in the recent past to achieve significant and ongoing curricular improvements" (p. 677).

Briggs (2007) emphasized the difference between teamwork collaboration and a community of practice engaged in continuous curriculum development. Teamwork collaboration is described as formal arrangements with clearly differentiated roles and responsibilities, clearly articulated goals and timelines, effective communication, and small group work to accomplish specific goals. Teamwork has an endpoint that produces a product or outcome. A community of practice centers around a domain of knowledge and interest; involves a community of people who care about the domain and who share expertise, responsibility and interest in developing frameworks, ideas, tools, information, and documents to improve practices within the domain. A community of practice is a continuous collaboration based on individual commitment and motivation with flexible roles, responsibilities, and levels of participation. This differentiation of perspectives on collaboration provides a lens through which to view the work of program renewal in teacher preparation described in this book.

The context for the renewal of the preservice teacher preparation program on which part of the discussion in this book is based initially required collaborative teamwork that was transformed into a community of practice through the approach used by the leadership team. Meeting new mandates and standards at a research-intensive university as required by the state department of education and the national accreditation agency presented serious challenges that were institutional, departmental, and programmatic. These challenges were systemic, cultural, ideological, social, and political. An example of an institutional challenge was new procedures and timelines for course and program approval for the university that did not fit with those set by the state department of education for the approval of teacher licensure programs. While the school of education as a unit was responsible for all teacher licensure programs, several programs were housed in the college of arts and sciences (art, music, and foreign language education). The general education and the subject matter preparation for all undergraduate licensure programs were within the purview of the college of arts and sciences. Additionally, some professional preparation courses were taught within the school of education, but not in the division of teacher education. Within the division, most courses were owned by individual faculty, and some faculty assumed personal ownership of specific credential programs. This meant that individual faculty could change course content and even redesign programs at their discretion. This situation was further complicated by a major ideological challenge within the field of teacher preparation whereby faculty often view themselves as subject matter experts (mathematics educators, science educators, etc.) rather than as teacher educators. Consequently, a limited number of faculty give attention to the scholarly literature on the preparation of classroom teachers. These factors have contributed to the abdication of responsibility for linking coursework with clinical experiences, and for monitoring candidates' progress in learning to teach.

Developing an approach for collaborative teamwork in the existing university context, school of education, and the department housing most of the teacher licensure programs required knowledge of teacher preparation program design, state requirements for program authorization and approval, and the requirements for national accreditation. A transition plan for revising existing teacher preparation programs to meet new mandates required a comparative analysis that would reveal the needed changes. Developing the approach, organizational structure, tools, and vision for collaborative teamwork was the responsibility of the facilitator for program renewal.

The general format for the collaborative teamwork was an explanation of an issue, challenge, or approach presented by the leadership team followed by open discussion by the faculty. During the open discussion, divergent perspectives and

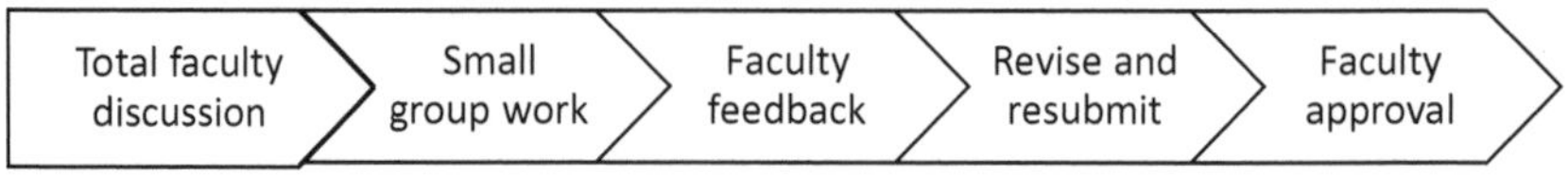

| Total faculty discussion | Small group work | Faculty feedback | Revise and resubmit | Faculty approval |

Collaborative teamwork involves collective participation and responsibility for teacher preparation, program decision making, and completing specific tasks for program design and improvement.

FIGURE 2.2 Collaborative teamwork

suggestions were sought, and informal consensus was encouraged. Following the open discussion, faculty were organized into small groups to complete specific tasks. Finished work was presented to the whole group for feedback. The small group revised and resubmitted the final product for faculty approval. This format for collaborative teamwork was followed for all substantive work of the department related to program renewal, including program revisions, modifications in handbooks and manuals; and the removal, development, and addition of new courses.

One example of the approach to collaborative teamwork is that of planning clinical experiences. The discussion of clinical experiences began with a presentation of the state and national requirements led by the leadership team. This presentation included the state department requirement of an early, middle, and culminating experience consisting of a specific number of hours. The presentation ended with a question about what candidates should learn at each level of the clinical experiences required by the state and the basis for such decisions. During the open discussion, as faculty made suggestions about what should be included in each level of clinical experiences, and a question about the relationship between the clinical experiences and the state and national standards was raised. A member of the leadership team developed a graphic into which faculty began to place the InTASC standards at each level of clinical experiences. Over the course of two meetings the faculty agreed on an organizational structure for clinical experiences, the standards that were to be met in each clinical experience, and an approach to monitoring candidates' progress towards competent teaching.

The approach to monitoring candidates' progress towards competent teaching was a set of ten key assessments based on each of the ten InTASC standards. The leadership team created a template for developing the key assessments. After feedback and approval of the template, the leadership team members each volunteered to work on developing a key assessment for one of the InTASC standards. Volunteers were invited to participate. Faculty with specific expertise who did not volunteer were asked to assist. Individuals from other departments with expertise in the areas being addressed were invited to contribute. These initial small groups formed by the leadership team members developed drafts of key assessments that were submitted to the faculty for review and feedback. These first draft key assessments were revised, and final products were submitted to the faculty for approval. The leadership team modeled the collaborative teamwork process and produced examples of key assessments that supported faculty small group work. Faculty were invited to volunteer for work in small groups on the remaining key assessments. A few faculty members in the teacher education department chose not to participate in the development of key assessments, to were part of the review and approval process. The process for review and approval by the faculty was followed for each of the key assessments.

A second example of collaborative teamwork was that for revising existing courses and developing new courses. A member of the leadership team created a table of all required courses across all credential programs. The table included the course number, title, number of units, brief course description, licensure areas that required each course, and the departmental location of the course. Existing courses not required under the new state mandate, as well as new course requirements, were identified in the table. Included in the table was a space for identifying the faculty leader for each course. The faculty reviewed the table and made corrections and suggestions for a process. The responsibility of the faculty leader was to form a small group for revising a course to meet new standards using a template developed by the leadership team and approved by the faculty. Forming small groups for course revisions was especially important given that most courses were used across two or more licensure areas and some courses were taught by faculty not in the department of teacher education or by adjuncts. Some adjuncts were invited to participate in course revisions and course development. All faculty in the teacher education department and coordinators for licensure programs in the college of arts and sciences participated in the course revision and development process.

Collaboration with Faculty and Staff Across Campus

The regular monthly meetings of the Teacher Education Coordinating Council (TECC) were the context for the teacher licensure program renewal. This context was chosen because participants included all faculty in teacher preparation, coordinators for teacher licensure areas in the college of arts and sciences, and representatives from other units in the school of education. Collaboration with faculty from other disciplines was built into the process at meetings for the TECC. However, the approach to collaborative teamwork used in this program renewal had not been a regular practice.

Collaborative teamwork supported coherence, continuity and consistency within licensure areas, and consistency across areas as appropriate. For example, courses across all licensure areas used the same format for revision and development, included a clinical experience assignment, applied technology, and addressed issues of diversity. All licensure areas included a course on ethical and legal issues in teaching. Middle, secondary, and K-12 licensure programs included a course on adolescent growth and development. Early childhood and elementary licensure programs included a course on child growth and development. Courses taught across different programs were made relevant for specific licensure areas through collaborative teamwork.

Collaborating with faculty in the college of arts and sciences, who were responsible for subject matter specializations, required more effort. This required the coordinators for each licensure program to meet with the appropriate departments in the college of arts and sciences. First, the faculty needed to decide what subject matter knowledge was required for teaching in each area of licensure. Then, this information needed to be shared with colleagues in arts and sciences to negotiate courses and course content framed to prepare candidates for teaching. In some instances, this meant adding and removing courses from subject majors and changing content in existing courses. The faculty developed a plan for the dialogue. Program coordinators assembled the appropriate documents to guide the collaboration, including standards for teacher content knowledge established by the appropriate professional organization (e.g., National Council for Teachers of English, National Council for Social Studies, National Council for Teachers of Mathematics, etc.), P-12 curriculum standards, and the state framework for content assessment in the appropriate subject matter area. Program coordinators scheduled meetings with the appropriate representatives from the unit in the college of arts and sciences. The appropriate documents were sent prior to the meeting to provide time for review and analysis.

During the meeting with arts and sciences faculty, it was explained that the school of education is responsible for verifying that each candidate recommended for licensure has met all state and national requirements, including the requirements for subject matter knowledge. This means providing evidence in the form of syllabi that include the standards and competencies supported by appropriate readings and course assignments, and candidates' performance on the assessment for content knowledge. Licensure program coordinators and content area representatives mapped standards and competencies to individual subject matter courses. Representatives were to identify readings and develop appropriate course assignments. Program coordinators kept notes on course modifications that were agreed on and provided written documentation for the representative following the meeting. Copies of the appropriately revised course syllabi were provided for program coordinators.

Many students at the local community college have an interest in the teaching profession. Local community college administrators and faculty often respond by designing a two-year course sequence that enables students to complete teacher licensure with a bachelor's degree in four years. However, state and national accreditation standards require that authorized providers assume responsibility for the subject matter and professional preparation of all candidates recommended to the state for licensure. It is important for teacher preparation providers to communicate and collaborate with community college faculty when significant changes are made in licensure requirements that impact community college students transferring to a teacher preparation program.

In this case, representatives from the teacher preparation program met with administrators and faculty at the community college using the same format as was used in meeting with representatives from the college of arts and sciences. This process was a bit more complicated given that the students from the local community college do not all plan to attend the same four-year university in the area. While licensure programs with different providers are required to meet the same standards, they do not all subscribe to the same program practices. For example, to be eligible to complete the program offered by one provider, students need to complete three required key assessments and the associated clinical experiences while attending community college. Other program providers in the area do not require key assessments structured in the same way as described in this book. Further, the related professional and subject matter courses required for addressing the appropriate standards and competencies supported with readings and assignments needed to be developed and aligned. Copies of syllabi for the sequence of professional and subject matter courses preparing candidates for a licensure program needed to be submitted to the teacher preparation faculty.

A significant challenge in the collaboration among university-based faculty and community college faculty relates to continuous program improvement and creating a community of practice. For example, findings from administering the key assessments to university-based candidates' revealed weakness in written communication skills. The policy on the administration of key assessments required blind scoring and faculty were not permitted to provide suggestions for improvement before or after submission; thus, candidates did not receive individual corrective feedback. The rubric used to score the key assessments did not provide direct feedback suggesting corrections. These practices were intentionally focused on producing an authentic indication of candidates' progress towards competent teaching. The teacher educators representing an authorized provider could not warrant that community college faculty followed these procedures, identified program areas in need of correction and took appropriate action.

The teacher preparation faculty decided to collaborate with the writing center to help candidates improve their competence in analytical writing. The facilitator for program renewal contacted the director of the writing center to solicit assistance. The director agreed to consider the request. A copy of the handbook for key assessments and submissions scored at each of the first three levels of the key assessment rubric were sent to the director. The director reviewed the documents and agreed to assist candidates who scored below proficient on any of the key assessments. Developing the candidates' analytical writing skills improved the ability to apply professional knowledge to practice and increased accuracy in assessing progress towards competent teaching. Thus, the writing center became part of preservice teacher preparation for candidates who were unable to score at the proficient level on the first submission of a key assessment. Students at the local community college do not have access to the university-based writing center.

Collaboration with Practitioners

It is essential that practitioners are involved in teacher preparation program renewal at the outset and that conversations are meaningful and productive. In the present example, the first conversation with practitioners regarding teacher preparation program renewal was by invitation to a dinner meeting at a local restaurant. Those in attendance were primarily school administrators with direct interaction with candidates and program completers. The conversation for the evening was framed by an overview of changes required by the state department of education and the national accrediting agency for educator preparation programs. After presentation of the overview, the group was organized for roundtable discussions by grade level and subject area facilitated by faculty with the appropriate expertise. The facilitator for program renewal ensured that the conversation was focused on specific questions or issues and that everyone had an opportunity to speak. The discussion was focused on the needs of schools and districts. The following questions focused the roundtable discussions:

1. What content knowledge do teachers need for helping students meet specific objectives for their grade level and subject area?
2. What pedagogical knowledge and skills are required for teachers to meet the needs of students at your school or in your district?
3. Are there particular ideas, concepts, or skills that should be included in teacher preparation coursework to help teacher candidates better understand students in your school or school district?
4. Is there anything else you would like to share that might improve teacher preparation to better meet the needs of students in your school or school district?

A report to the whole group followed the roundtable discussion. Afterwards, participants shared additional ideas and clarification. A follow-up survey was sent to all participants who attended the meeting, as well as those who were invited but were unable to attend. Data from the meeting and the survey were compiled and shared with the faculty for discussion and application in the program renewal process. Several weeks later a second meeting was held with the same practitioners to share the changes made in the program and to explain how the issues raised at the first meeting were incorporated into the program. This was an especially important process.

The initial meetings with practitioners from across schools and school districts served multiple purposes. The meetings provided input from practitioners that helped teacher educators in identifying areas of teacher preparation programs that needed improvement and problems of practice that needed to be addressed. The dialogue among teacher educators and practitioners helped build mutual respect and trust where practitioners gained confidence in academically based teacher preparation and were more likely to employ program completers. Administrators familiar with the teacher preparation program can advocate for it with colleagues in their schools and school districts.

Developing a partnership with schools and school districts requires collaborative teamwork. This is especially true if partnerships are to provide reciprocal benefit for participants. The potential benefits are numerous. For example, administrators benefit from knowing about new requirements for licensure and new mandates for teacher preparation. This information helps administrators understand how to support novice teachers. The benefit for candidates and preservice teacher preparation is opportunities for observation and application of academic knowledge in authentic classroom settings and access to the knowledge of practice that has been acquired by the mentor teachers. The mentor teachers benefit from the focus of attention on practice while providing guidance for candidates and through gaining access to knowledge from the preservice teacher preparation program. Students benefit from the increased attention to their needs and responses to the classroom context.

Often, developing a comprehensive plan for a collaborative partnership begins at the school district level. In the example of this program renewal, contact with the local urban school district began with the associate superintendent responsible for the curriculum and teacher professional development. A meeting was scheduled with the associate superintendent and department staff for a presentation describing the program renewal process, the redesigned preservice teacher preparation program, the vision for clinical experiences, and the collaboration necessary for implementation. The associate superintendent and staff identified several schools that might be suitable and interested in such a collaboration.

Collaborative teamwork with partners requires developing shared understanding of the school context, the teacher preparation program, common goals, and reciprocal benefit. The first meeting at the potential partner school included the leadership team for the school and the leadership team for the teacher preparation program renewal. The school leadership team described the school and shared handouts of information provided to parents and the community. The teacher preparation leadership team made a formal PowerPoint presentation that provided an overview of the entire preservice teacher preparation program including the philosophical stance, theoretical perspective on learning to teach, epistemic practices, course structure, monitoring and assessment, and vision for clinical experiences. The two teams discussed how the school staff and teacher preparation faculty might collaborate. The principal invited the teacher preparation leadership team to make a short 10-minute presentation at the next school staff meeting. Afterwards, the principal identified a small group of teachers to meet with faculty to develop a detailed plan for collaborative teamwork that would be presented to the principal for final approval.

The teacher preparation leadership team met with the group of teachers identified by the principal. At the first meeting, the teachers discussed the school and their work as classroom teachers. The teacher preparation leadership team provided a formal overview of the preservice teacher preparation program comparable to that provided for the school leadership team. The teachers discussed their perception of the school capacity for engaging in the type of collaborative teamwork described by the teacher preparation leadership team.

At the second partner school, teachers chose to work with candidates in clinical experiences at levels I and II. These levels were heavily focused on observation, documentation, and interpretation of teaching practices based on academic knowledge from coursework with limited interaction with students. Teachers identified the specific roles they would assume in organizing, monitoring, and providing feedback for clinical experiences in levels I and II that were consistent with the program design. The teachers requested training for modeling the teaching practices candidates were to observe for the assigned key assessments.

Teachers at the third partner school preferred levels III and IV that focused more on teaching and interacting with students, while teachers at other schools thought it important for candidates to remain in one school for all four levels of the clinical experience. Such variations in teachers' preferences were accommodated through collaborative teamwork.

During the first year of implementation, teachers at all the schools indicated that they personally benefited from participating in the experiences for preservice teachers through creating contexts and situations for candidates to complete key assessments and through discussions about what was being learned in university coursework for preservice teacher preparation. For example, one teacher explained how much she had learned about her students from candidates completing the key assessment examining the social dynamics in a small group and determining what facilitated or thwarted task completion. Another teacher discussed what she learned about supporting an isolated student when interviewed by a candidate completing a key assessment focused on this issue.

The Transition to a Community of Practice

The collaborative teamwork for program renewal involving whole faculty dialogue, consensus building, and faculty approval of small group work products provided the socialization for developing a community of practice. Key assessments provided a tool for monitoring candidates' progress towards competent teaching and for faculty engagement in continuous program improvement. The emergence of a community of practice focused on continuous program improvement was most evident in the faculty conversation after the first set of submissions for a key assessment were scored. In the analysis of candidates' responses on the key assessment faculty noticed wide variations in analytical writing skills. Candidates scoring below proficient tended to struggle the most with analytical writing skills. The faculty discussed options for supporting candidates in developing their writing skills.

Over time, scoring submissions for the key assessments led to faculty making adjustments in the handbook that included changes in language usage for clarity, in instruction for protocols to improve communication and understanding, in course sequence for better alignment with key assessments, and in readings and course assignments to improve professional preparation and performance on the key assessments.

Conclusion

The design or renewal and continuous improvement of preservice teacher preparation require insightful and responsive leadership, collective responsibility, collaborative teamwork, and the development of a community of practice. The framework employed in this book provides the elements of program design and the indicators of quality that guide the collaborative teamwork and the work in a community of practice. Leadership provides the context, information, and tools that enable and support full participation, access to the knowledge distributed among the faculty, consensus building, collaborative teamwork, and the development of a community of practice. In assuming collective responsibility, the whole faculty reached consensus and approved each component of the program and each product of collaborative teamwork. In collaborative teamwork, small groups of faculty took responsibility for specific tasks that were to be completed such as course development or revision, and the design of specific key assessments. During the process of implementing the new program design or program renewal, the faculty collective responsibility and collaborative teamwork evolved into a community of practice concerned with continuous program improvement.

References

Beck, C. & Kosnik, C. (2002). Professors and the practicum: Involvement of university faculty in preservice practicum supervision. *Journal of Teacher Education*, 53 (1), 6–19.

Briggs, C. L. (2007). Curriculum collaboration: A key to continuous program renewal. *The Journal of Higher Education*, 78 (6), 676–711.

Ginsberg, R. & Rhodes, L. K. (2003). University faculty in partner schools. *Journal of Teacher Education*, 54 (2), 150–162.

National Center for Education Statistics (2013). *The nation's report card: Trends in academic progress 2012*. Washington, DC: Institute for Education Sciences, United States Department of Education.

National Center for Education Statistics (2019). *The nation's report card: Results from 2019 mathematics and reading*. Washington, DC: Institute for Education Sciences, United States Department of Education.

Quinlan, K. M. & Akerlind G. S. (2000). Factors affecting departmental peer collaboration for faculty development: Two cases in context. *Higher Education*, 40 (1), 23–52.

Shields, C. M. (2011). Transformative leadership: An introduction. Transformative Leadership: A Reader, *Counterpoints*, 409, 1–17.

Wilkins, E. A., Young, A., & Sterner, S. (2009). An examination of institutional reports: Use of data for program improvement. *Action in Teacher Education*, 31 (1), 14–23.

Wolsey, T. D., Young, J. R., Scales, R. Q., Scales, W. D., Lenski, S., Yoder, K. K., Wold, L., Smetana, L., Grisham, D. L. & Ganske, K. (2013). An examination of teacher education in literacy instruction and candidate perceptions of their learned literacy practices. *Action in Teacher Education*, 35, 204–222.

3

FRAMEWORK FOR PROGRAM DESIGN

Introduction

Recent initiatives for redesigning preservice teacher preparation programs have favored teacher residency approaches. Most major cities across the United States have an urban teacher residency initiative. Many residency programs are included in a consortium or research project such as Teachers for a New Era (TNE), National Center for Teacher Residency (NCTR), and Urban Teacher Residency United (UTRU). These residency approaches are focused on preparing teachers for urban, low-income, and underserved schools with challenges in the recruitment and retention of competent and experienced teachers. In addition, some teacher residency programs focus on teacher shortages in mathematics, science, and special education. Most residency programs emphasize the recruitment and preparation of candidates who are members of traditionally underserved groups.

The approach employed in residency programs reflects some of the structural aspects of a medical residency in that candidates engage in an apprenticeship with an experienced and competent teacher for one year or longer. In some programs, candidates co-teach with a mentor teacher. In other programs, candidates serve as the teacher of record under the supervision of a mentor teacher who provides regular observation and feedback (coaching). Emphasis is placed on the recruitment and training of highly qualified teachers as mentors and coaches.

Each teacher residency initiative has a program design framework. Teachers for a New Era identified three program design principles indicating that programs should be guided by:

- a respect for evidence,
- full engagement of faculty in the arts and sciences, and

- understanding education as "an academically taught clinical practice profession."
  (Teachers for a New Era, 2001)

The National Center for Teacher Residencies identified five components for program design that include:

1. recruitment and selection,
2. coursework and seminars,
3. coaching and feedback,
4. assessment and evaluation, and
5. the school and school system. *(www.nctresidencies.org)*

The Urban Teacher Residency United (UTRU), Kansas City Urban Residency program focused on blending theory and practice in coursework and clinical experiences while emphasizing "issues of equity, data driven instruction, literacy instruction across all content areas, culturally relevant instruction, implementation of college and career readiness standards, Missouri standards, teacher evaluation framework, and Mo state competencies for teacher education" (Kansas City Teacher Residency Partner Prospectus, 2015). Each residency initiative is focused on preparing teachers for urban and underserved students, emphasizes clinically based practices in collaboration with partner schools, and employs a cognitive apprenticeship approach involving mentor teachers as models of good teaching practice. Cognitive apprenticeship is at the heart of traditional practices in preservice teacher preparation.

Teacher educators assume responsibility as *architects of the teaching profession* in the process of designing teacher preparation programs and determining the knowledge base for teaching and teacher preparation. The discussion in this chapter presents a program design framework for academically based and clinically grounded preservice teacher preparation that supports this responsibility. This framework has two major parts—conceptual elements and structural elements (Figure 3.1). The conceptual elements include a philosophical stance, theoretical perspective on learning to teach, professional knowledge and skills, and epistemic practices. The structural elements include admission practices, alignment of courses and clinical experiences, school partnerships, assessment of professional knowledge and skills, and program evaluation. This design framework is based on actual cases of program redesign engaged by faculty at four different universities; however, this is not a research report or a detailed account of the collaborative practices of the facilitators or the faculty. Many of the practices and protocols described are based on authentic artifacts from these redesign experiences. Some examples and graphics in this chapter and in other parts of this book have been created to facilitate understanding and application of the framework. This framework is intended to facilitate designing and improving teacher preparation programs with different purposes, providers, and contexts.

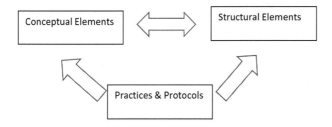

The conceptual and structural elements in a teacher preparation program are reciprocal and are supported by correlated practices and protocols.

FIGURE 3.1 Teacher preparation program design

Program Conceptual Elements

This framework has four conceptual elements: philosophical stance, theoretical perspective, professional knowledge and skills, and epistemic practices. The philosophical stance or purpose for a preservice program is a clearly articulated statement of the general goals, ideals, and values that are evident in program practices. The theoretical perspective is an explanation of the process for learning to teach that frames the development of learning experiences for courses and clinical experiences, and the assessment of progress toward competent teaching. Professional knowledge and skills are the subject matter for teaching practices and teacher preparation. Epistemic practices grounded in the philosophical stance and theoretical perspective for the teacher preparation program are the rituals and routines that develop the habits of mind and professional practices that support competent teaching.

Philosophical Stance

A philosophical stance is a clearly-delineated statement of purpose that identifies the characteristics of the target population for recruitment into a preservice teacher preparation program, the essence of what candidates are expected to learn and be able to do; and the impact of the preparation on a clearly identified target population of P-12 students, the students' communities, and the larger society. The philosophical stance frames the approaches and practices in the preservice teacher preparation program related to recruitment, curriculum design, and learning experiences and assignments in courses and clinical experiences. The following is one example of a philosophical stance.

THE PERCY JULIAN PRESERVICE TEACHER PREPARATION PROGRAM

The primary focus of the Percy Julian Preservice Teacher Preparation Program is to recruit and prepare science teachers from urban and rural communities who are committed to teaching secondary science for students living in these communities. Teacher candidates admitted into the Percy Julian Preservice Teacher Preparation Program are required to demonstrate deep knowledge of subject matter, including the structure of the discipline, application of subject matter knowledge in everyday life and to practice in occupations and professions. Upon completing the teacher preparation program, candidates are expected to demonstrate the ability to apply to practice the principles of *relevance* and *cognition* in supporting urban and rural secondary students' learning science. The teaching practices of program completers are expected to provide secondary students with foundational disciplinary literacy, including subject matter knowledge, and disciplinary practices and skills that promote interest in advanced study and careers in science.

The name of the Percy Julian Science Teacher Preparation Program embodies its philosophical stance. Percy Julian (1899–1975), the grandson of former slaves, was born in Montgomery, Alabama and earned a master's degree in Chemistry at Harvard University in 1923. Percy Julian faced adversity and racial oppression on his journey to becoming a celebrated research chemist who pioneered the synthesis of medicinal drugs from plants. The Percy Julian Science Teacher Preparation Program recruits and prepares teacher candidates who have lived in conditions where they experienced or observed challenges related to those of Percy Julian. These teacher candidates are prepared to teach secondary students with background experiences that mirror their own. In the preservice teacher preparation program, candidates build upon their insider knowledge through the application of the principles of relevance and cognition.

The *principle of relevance* indicates that the quality of learning in depth and breadth is directly proportionate to the connections made between new knowledge and what the learner knows, has experienced, and values. Application of the principle of relevance incorporates deep knowledge of specific learners, learning, subject matter, and pedagogy in making new knowledge accessible and meaningful for the learners being taught. The knowledge and experience candidates bring to the preservice program when incorporated into professional preparation enables candidates to demonstrate the ability to apply the principle of relevance after program completion.

The principle of relevance and the principle of cognition are interdependent. The *principle of cognition* refers to internal mental processes that enable the use of language to express the conceptualization of ideas for which a mental image is visualized, and an organized mental or cognitive schema is developed (Piaget, 1953; Vygotsky, 1978). The connection between new knowledge and what the learner knows, has experienced, and values supports the development of mental images and cognitive schema. In turn, existing mental images and cognitive schema support or impede access to new knowledge.

The *application of academic knowledge to practice* in preservice preparation, teaching, and student learning is a signature feature in the philosophical stance for the Percy Julian Science Teacher Preparation Program. Candidates learn to apply knowledge to practice from multiple sources during their preservice program and to demonstrate the ability to apply academic knowledge to practice as professionals in the field. Students taught by program completers learn to apply their knowledge of science in their everyday lives and to consider advanced study and careers in science. This is an example of the design and application of a philosophical stance.

Theoretical Perspective on Learning Teaching

The theoretical perspective in teacher preparation program design explains the process of student learning, informs teaching practices, and explains the process of learning to teach, including systematic approaches in teaching and teacher preparation. Yilmaz (2008) argued that: "learning theories are indispensable for effective and pedagogically meaningful instructional practices" (p. 161). Planning and enacting powerful learning experiences require intentionally coordinated, integrated, and sequential actions. The theoretical perspective supports coherence, continuity, and consistency in this process. Teacher preparation is a process that enables candidates to develop and apply professional knowledge to practice for facilitating student learning. The theoretical perspective explains and guides this process.

In program design, the theoretical perspective on learning to teach is based on an understanding of the *teaching process* and the cognitive engagement and social arrangements that enable learning to teach. The two theoretical perspectives that most often inform preservice teacher preparation are cognitivism and constructivism. These perspectives are described in the discussion that follows.

Cognitivist Perspectives

Cognitivist perspectives employed in teaching and learning to teach are focused on *mental processes* that connect new knowledge with prior knowledge and experience. These mental processes focus on understanding, remembering, and applying new knowledge. Levin (1986) identified four cognitive principles for application to instruction. First, different learning strategies serve different cognitive purposes. These different cognitive purposes include understanding, remembering, and applying. Strategies for remembering may not support understanding and applying.

Strategies for understanding may not support remembering and applying. These cognitive processes of understanding, remembering, and applying are interrelated for supporting learning. Second, effective learning strategies should have identifiable components. The cognitive processes supported by each component are clearly identified. Each learning activity targets the processing of specific variables and operations such as prior knowledge or elaboration of new knowledge. Third, learning strategies are considered in relation to students' knowledge and skills, and a match between strategy and learner characteristics is required. Fourth, learning strategies thought to be effective require empirical validation. Levin (1986) pointed out that "even theoretically sound and empirically tested learning strategies require classroom validation before they can be prescribed for classroom use" (p. 13).

Yilmaz (2011) provided examples of instructional approaches consistent with a cognitivist theoretical perspective that include cognitive apprenticeship, reciprocal teaching, anchor instruction, and inquiry learning. The cognitive apprenticeship involves modeling, coaching, articulation, reflection, and exploration. Reciprocal teaching employs modeling, coaching, scaffolding, and fading. Anchor instruction uses strategies such as case studies or problem situations. Inquiry learning uses a scientific inquiry method to promote higher-order thinking.

In preservice teacher preparation, the cognitivist theoretical perspective is most evident in student teaching, internships, and residencies where an apprenticeship approach is employed (Torrez & Krebs, 2020; McDiarmid & Caprino, 2018). In this approach, teaching is often focused on performance. Faculty attempt to place candidates with teachers who model *good teaching practices*. Candidates are expected to replicate their mentor's practices. The relationship between the mentor teacher and the candidate is that of co-teaching or coaching with frequent feedback and support.

The cognitive apprenticeship approach for learning to teach has met with significant challenges that are often unresolved. First, the expectation for replicating existing teaching practices often contributes to discontinuity between academic knowledge gained in professional courses and the intuitive and idiosyncratic practices often found in classroom teaching. Second, replicating the practices of mentor teachers raises questions about the depth of understanding candidates develop that is applicable and transferable for teaching students with different characteristics and in different school settings. It is highly unlikely that one classroom includes all the possible variations in individual student characteristics and developmental needs. Further, very few models of good teaching practice are identified in schools with a high percentage of underserved students. The good teaching practices employed in suburban schools do not provide the same benefit for students from urban and rural communities as for white middle-class students. The best explanation for this variation in outcomes when using the same teaching practices for students with different cultural and experiential backgrounds is based on the principles of relevance and cognition described in the philosophical stance for the Percy Julian teacher preparation program.

Constructivist Perspectives

The constructivist perspectives on learning are student-centered and focused on active meaning-making and continuously expanding cognitive schemas by building upon and enhancing understanding of prior knowledge and experience. The principle of continuity that refers to a continuous and progressive restructuring of understanding through experience is central in the constructivist perspective. In the constructivist perspective, declarative knowledge and procedural knowledge are interrelated, but different and require different approaches. According to Kumar (2006), declarative knowledge is information about a phenomenon that is often descriptive or explanatory. Procedural knowledge presents a sequence of actions for the application of declarative knowledge to practice. The development of procedural knowledge requires a higher level of cognitive processing and analytical reasoning for comprehension and application.

Cognitivist and constructivist perspectives share pedagogical practices such as coaching, modeling, and scaffolding and instructional approaches such as inquiry learning and problem-based instruction. However, there are differences in purpose and strategies. According to Kumar (2006), constructivism employs:

> task-oriented learning activities where learners are exposed to a spectrum of cognitive processes involving comprehending, applying, creating, elaborating, managing, critiquing, and cross-referencing the body of organized prerequisite basic declarative knowledge to build upon new extended/connected knowledge structures.
>
> *(p. 258)*

Constructivist teaching practices are concerned with a teaching and learning cycle and process. In contrast, traditional cognitivist teaching practices and learning to teach are concerned with teaching and learning cognitive strategies focused on understanding and remembering new information, practices, and procedures. Mayer (2001) pointed out that:

> Cognitive strategies are cognitive processes that the learner intentionally performs to influence learning and cognition. Examples include basic processes such as using a rehearsal strategy to memorize a list and metacognitive strategies such as recognizing whether one comprehends a passage.
>
> *(p. 86)*

Hollins (2011) introduced *teaching as an interpretive practice/process* (Figure 3.2) as an alternative to the traditional *cognitive apprenticeship* approach. This new approach employs a *mediated learning* modality based on a constructivist theoretical perspective. This approach is supported by epistemic practices that involve a sequence of focused inquiry, directed observation, and guided practice that foster

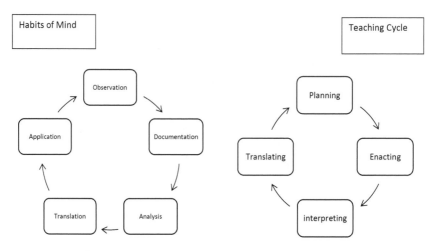

FIGURE 3.2 Teaching as an interpretive practice/process

the habits of mind characterized by the process of observation, documentation, analysis, translation, and application of new insights to practice. The epistemic practices and habits of mind inform the teaching cycle that includes planning, enacting, interpreting, and translating students' responses to learning experiences for subsequent planning that improves learning outcomes. Candidates engage in focused inquiry in their courses where they develop the professional knowledge for teaching. Early clinical experiences provide opportunities for directed observation linking academic professional knowledge to classroom and school practices. Guided practice in clinical experiences provides opportunities for candidates to translate declarative knowledge from coursework to procedural knowledge for classroom teaching. This approach is elaborated in Chapter 6 in the discussion of clinical experiences.

Professional Knowledge and Skills

Professional knowledge and skills for preservice teacher preparation come from many different sources including state and national accreditation standards, professional organizations, research, scholarly literature, and standards provided by the Interstate Teacher Assessment and Support Consortium (InTASC). Professional knowledge and skills from these different sources are applicable in course content when used to develop specific objectives; and identify knowledge and learning experiences related to the subject matter that is the focus of the course. Further, meaningful course content addresses relevant research and theory, as well as observations and feedback from practitioners in the field concerned with students' learning needs and problems of practice (Hollins, 2011).

Candidates develop the knowledge and skills for teaching through academic work that supports deep knowledge of learners, learning, pedagogy, subject matter, and professional responsibility. Professional knowledge includes theory, research, and application to practice. Declarative and procedural knowledge are correlated through course assignments and clinical experiences. Professional knowledge is cumulative, increasingly complex, and developmentally sequenced across courses and clinical experiences to ensure coherence and continuity across the teacher preparation process.

Knowledge of learners includes child and adolescent growth and development, knowledge of the culture and community setting in which students grow and develop, and societal conditions and values that impact students' communities and life experiences. Candidates learn how to develop deep knowledge of specific individuals and groups of students taught in the classroom and how to monitor and assess individual growth and development in all areas academic, psychological, physical, and social.

Knowledge of learning emphasizes the understanding and application of theories of learning and motivation, accommodation for variations in academic and intellectual development, language learning and development, and social skills development. Candidates learn how to create a social context for learning and to ensure that each student feels comfortable and supported.

Candidates develop extensive procedural knowledge for facilitating student learning, planning instruction, developing learning experiences, assessing students' progress, and evaluating learning experiences. Knowledge of pedagogy includes understanding general practices for facilitating learning applied across subject matter areas; pedagogy derived from discipline-specific practices; and the ability to frame the curriculum and use pedagogical approaches that benefit students from different cultural and experiential backgrounds. Candidates develop a deep understanding of the relationship among learner characteristics, pedagogical practices, and learning outcomes.

Knowledge of subject matter includes understanding discipline-specific practices, the structure of the discipline, the interrelationship among big ideas, and how new knowledge is generated, validated, and communicated. Framing the curriculum is a complex process that involves positioning, focusing, and contextualizing. Framing the curriculum for meaningful and productive learning requires addressing the basic principles of value, relevance, and applicability. The value principle in teaching refers to the factor in instruction that appeals to something the learner finds highly desirable and potentially beneficial. The applicability principle refers to the learner's perception of the usefulness of the new knowledge or skill. Relevance is the connection between the new knowledge and what the learner knows, has experienced, and values. These and other concepts related to curriculum framing are further elaborated in Chapter 6.

Professional responsibility includes:

- the appropriate use of professional knowledge and skills for the benefit of students, parents, the community and the profession;

- the ethical use, maintenance, and protection of information about students and families and with regard for privacy rights;
- knowledge of ethical and legal requirements for professional practice;
- continuous improvement of teaching practices through regular professional development; and
- active participation in and contribution to advancing the profession.

Candidates develop this knowledge through coursework, attending school and district level meetings for teachers, and attending statewide and national conferences held by organizations for teachers.

Epistemic Practices

Epistemic practices are purposefully developed sequences of interrelated and repetitive actions that establish routines; create order and predictability; and develop habits of mind and behaviors that increase accuracy and efficiency in an approach, completing a task, and achieving a goal or objective. In teaching and learning teaching, epistemic practices provide a scaffold for developing deep understanding of the relationship among pedagogical practices, subject matter, learning, learners, and learning outcomes.

An example of epistemic practices in preservice teacher preparation is a sequence of interrelated and repetitive actions that include focused inquiry, directed observation, and guided practice. Focused inquiry is an approach to gaining academic knowledge for professional practice through coursework, independent investigations, and observations. Directed observation is the careful documentation and analysis of knowledge from focused inquiry applied to practice in an authentic setting. Guided practice is the direct application of knowledge from focused inquiry in an authentic setting with guidance and feedback from a more experienced mentor. Guided practice can occur in a short clinical experience, during student teaching, or during a year-long internship or residency. When candidates engage in this sequence of interrelated and repetitive actions they are learning the habits of mind and behaviors associated with expert teaching that include the application of professional knowledge to practice; the continuous observation, documentation, and analysis of students' responses to learning experiences; and collaboration with more knowledgeable and experienced colleagues. These epistemic practices enable the candidate to construct deep knowledge of the application of theory to practice and the relationship among pedagogical practices, subject matter, learning, learners, and learning outcomes.

An example of the application of epistemic practices in classroom teaching is using discipline-specific practices as instructional approaches. Historical inquiry can be used as an approach to teaching middle and secondary history. Students learn the disciplinary practices of historians including how to critique and develop a historical narrative. Understanding how to critique a historical narrative includes knowledge of the practices for document analysis, sourcing, contextualizing, and corroborating evidence. Historical inquiry for constructing a historical narrative includes determining a focus such as a question, issue, or event; planning the investigation (stating the purpose, identifying data and sources for evidence); gathering and analyzing data and sources of evidence; and writing a narrative. The purpose for using historical inquiry as an epistemic practice is multi-dimensional including developing specific habits of mind related to the analysis of evidence from different sources, developing a deep understanding of critical issues from the past, understanding the work of professional historians, and preserving a democratic society through developing citizens who are less vulnerable to the influences of conspiracy theories and propaganda.

In sum, the use of epistemic practices to develop specific habits of mind is important for teaching and learning among candidates, teachers, and students. Using epistemic practices in preservice teacher preparation provides a continuous scaffold for the systematic analysis of teaching, planning learning experiences, and solving problems related to student learning and development for candidates and cooperating teachers. Establishing routines and predictability through epistemic practices in classroom teaching increases access to deep knowledge and self-regulation for students from diverse cultural and experiential backgrounds and those with special needs.

The concept of epistemic practices is quite different from that of "core practices" or "high-leverage practices" in purpose and theoretical perspective. The purpose of core practices is to establish a set of basic practices and routines that are essential for competent teaching used across disciplines and contexts. *Eliciting students' thinking* is an example of a core practice (McDonald et al., 2013). All teacher candidates are expected to develop and demonstrate competence in these basic practices and routines (Ball & Forzani, 2009). A cognitivist theoretical perspective guides practices in teacher preparation for developing procedural knowledge related to core teaching practices. According to Ball and Forzani (2009):

> Performing these activities effectively is intricate work. Professional training should be to help teachers learn to enact these tasks skillfully. Such training would involve seeing examples of each task, learning to dissect and analyze the work, watching demonstrations, and then practicing under close supervision and with detailed coaching aimed at fostering improvement.
>
> *(pp. 497–498)*

In contrast, epistemic practices are based on a constructivist theoretical perspective on learning to teach that engages candidates in experiences for developing the habits of mind, procedures and routines that inform decision-making for planning instruction and creating a social context for learning.

Structural Elements in Preservice Teacher Preparation Programs

Structural elements in preservice teacher preparation programs are those parts that are specifically arranged and organized to support the conceptual elements. The structural elements in this discussion include admission practices, the arrangement and relationship among courses and clinical experiences, assessment of candidates' professional knowledge and skills, and program evaluation. These structural elements are interrelated and interdependent. These are the working parts of the preservice program that operationalize the conceptual elements. Persons are admitted into the preservice program based on discernible attributes consistent with the philosophical stance and theoretical perspective for the program, and the propensity for participating in the epistemic practices. The philosophical stance and theoretical perspective for the program frame learning in courses and clinical experiences, incorporate professional knowledge and its application through epistemic practices. The arrangement of courses and clinical experiences support the application of theory to practice. The assessment of professional knowledge and skills documents candidates' progress towards competent teaching consistent with the philosophical stance for the program. Programmatic assessment provides evidence that the program achieves its goals and objectives and identifies areas for growth and development.

Program Admission Practices

Declining enrollment in preservice teacher preparation is a major concern for teacher educators and schools of education. A recent report from the Center for American Progress revealed that there were one-third fewer students enrolled in university-based teacher preparation programs in 2018 than in 2010, and that the percentage of students completing these programs dropped by 28 points. There was a slight drop in areas of mathematics and science. However, enrollment in alternative teacher preparation programs increased by 40%. There was an increase of 30% in teachers earning credentials for teaching English language learners and bilingual education. Shortages of teachers for special education, high school mathematics and science, and teachers from underrepresented groups continue. These data provide incentives for developing well-designed and trustworthy teacher preparation programs that recruit and prepare teachers whose students from all cultural and experiential backgrounds consistently meet expectations for grade level and subject area.

Accomplishing the purpose described in the philosophical stance is significantly influenced by the attributes and characteristics of prospective teachers admitted into the teacher preparation program, including their academic preparation, attitudes, beliefs, experiences, and values (Caskey, Peterson, & Temple, 2001; Falkenberg, 2010). The philosophical stance for the Percy Julian Science Teacher Preparation Program previously discussed in this chapter clearly identifies the target population for recruitment and admission—individuals with deep knowledge of science (including disciplinary practices and everyday applications), from urban and rural backgrounds, interested in teaching high school students with background experiences similar to their own, and who are interested in preparing the next generation for careers in science. An important attitude for the target population of prospective teachers is a commitment to science, science teaching, and facilitating learning for urban or rural students. Those admitted into the Percy Julian Science Teacher Preparation Program are convinced that when given high quality opportunities for learning, urban and rural students will excel in science. Prospective teachers' experiential backgrounds in urban or rural settings provide insider knowledge regarding the experiences and values of the youth who will become their students. In the preservice program, candidates learn to apply their insider knowledge in designing meaningful and productive learning experiences and framing curriculum content for their students.

The recruitment of prospective teachers for the Percy Julian Science Teacher Preparation Program is framed by the philosophical stance. The philosophical stance is used to generate an easy to remember tagline that appears on all materials advertising and describing the program such as: "Preparing teachers for the next generation of science professionals." Qualifications for admission into the teacher preparation program, key features and the expected impact of the teacher preparation program are made explicit in the initial advertising or recruitment materials. Subsequent recruitment materials include testimonials from program graduates and employers. Recruitment materials are distributed in various locations frequented by the target population, including urban and rural high schools, urban and rural community organizations and businesses, community colleges, and undergraduate programs at four-year colleges and universities.

Identifying and selecting candidates with dispositions aligned with the philosophical stance is an important, but complex process. Shiveley and Misco (2010) developed a four-step process for determining an appropriate approach for assessing prospective candidates' dispositions, including defining dispositions, operationalizing the definition, identifying strategies for assessment, and collecting and analyzing data. The assessment of dispositions and beliefs is important for determining the suitability for teaching in different school and classroom settings. Aragon, Culpepper, McKee, and Perkins (2014) "examines the relationship between preservice teachers' beliefs pertaining to diversity and urban schooling and how these inclinations contribute to a commitment to teaching urban students" (p. 543). An important finding from this investigation is that "preservice teachers who prefer suburban over urban schools tended to report agreement with fewer beliefs that are supportive of working with diverse students" (p. 562). This finding is consistent with that of Schmid (2018), in which high performing teachers in low achieving schools believed that "all students could and would learn, and that student learning was a direct reflection of their teaching" (p. 1). Aragon et al., (2014) used a survey at the beginning of the preservice teacher preparation program that when analyzed provided a profile of the beliefs of candidates. This survey can be used as part of the selection and admission process for preservice teacher preparation.

The process for selection and admission into the Percy Julian Science Teacher Preparation Program requires applicants to demonstrate deep knowledge of science, commitment to promoting the understanding and application of knowledge of science, personal experience in urban or rural communities, and a belief that high quality learning experiences will enable urban and rural students to prepare for careers in science. Applicants will demonstrate the attitudes, experience, and knowledge required for admission to the Percy Julian Science Teacher Preparation Program by responding to a prompt for a two-page single spaced essay to be submitted with the application and responding to five questions in a 5-member group in person interview. The two-page unsupervised essay questions provide opportunities for applicants to demonstrate knowledge of science and its application. The small group interview questions provide evidence of applicants' attitudes, beliefs, experiences, and values.

Sample prompts for the two-page essay are:

(A) Explain how Percy Julian's pioneering work in the chemical synthesis of medicinal drugs such as cortisone, steroids, and birth control pills can be used to help students understand the application of specific principles of chemistry.
(B) Explain how Percy Julian's work can be used to help students understand the relationship between chemistry and biology.

Sample questions for the small group interview are:

(A) The United States is becoming increasingly dependent on countries like India to supply much needed human resources in STEM areas. How do you explain the shortage of STEM professionals in the United States?
(B) What do you believe contributes to the differences in education outcomes in India and the United States related to students gaining knowledge of science?
(C) To what extent are classroom teachers responsible for preparing the next generation of science professionals in the United States?
(D) Describe at least one major challenge that existed in the urban or rural community where you lived that required deep knowledge of science and community support to address?
(E) If you were a teacher in this community how would you prepare your students to understand and address this challenge?

Alignment across Courses and Clinical Experiences

The arrangement of courses and clinical experiences, including the relationship among courses and between courses and clinical experiences, supports the application of theory to practice. In preservice programs characterized by coherence, continuity, and consistency, courses are interrelated, developmentally sequenced, and purposefully aligned with clinical experiences to provide candidates with opportunities for making observations and engaging in guided practice that directly relates to the focused inquiry in courses (Darling-Hammond, 2006). These experiences in courses and clinical experiences address four areas of professional knowledge:

- knowledge of theories of learning and of learning cycles;
- knowledge of learners' growth and development, and of the cultural and experiential backgrounds of specific learners;
- knowledge of subject matter and how to frame it to connect with learners' development, cultural and experiential backgrounds; and
- knowledge of general pedagogical practices that cut across subject matter areas, discipline-specific pedagogy, and teaching cycles.

The content in courses and clinical experiences is guided by research and theory in the field; identifiable and persistent problems of practice; and standards set by professional organizations (including InTASC), state departments of education, and national accreditation agencies. The use of this information to design courses and clinical experiences varies across faculties and preservice programs. However, course alignment and integration with clinical experiences require a purposeful and systematic approach. For example, courses with specific objectives enacted through readings, observations, application, and other experiences enable candidates to develop deep knowledge of the relationship between theory and practice. Observations and application of academic knowledge are completed during guided practice supervised by teacher educators and experienced practitioners in the field.

Competent teaching is developed through academic and clinical experiences that are developmentally sequenced such that candidates' understanding of professional knowledge and skills is comprehensive, cumulative, and increasingly complex (see Chapter 5). The InTASC standards are developmentally sequenced and can be used to guide the sequencing of courses and clinical experiences (see Chapter 6). A course sequence can be developed based on the relationship among course objectives, readings, and assignments.

School Partnerships

Learning to teach requires observation of *teacher facilitated* student learning and guided practice in *facilitating* student learning in authentic school settings. The most appropriate authentic settings include diversity among students related to culture, race, social class, abilities, and needs. These schools are representative, rather than exemplary, to provide opportunities for observing the challenges and successes of teaching. Candidates have opportunities to apply the professional knowledge and skills, habits of mind and protocols learned through academic experiences, and to collaborate with teachers and faculty in addressing real problems of practice (Thompson, Hagenah, Lohwasser, & Laxton, 2015). This type of purposeful collaboration is most often embedded in partnerships that embrace shared responsibility for the preparation of preservice teachers, mutual benefit for the development of teaching practices, and for advancing the teaching profession. This type of partnership requires purposeful collaboration, shared understanding of goals and practices, joint productive activity, and mutual or reciprocal benefit related to improving preservice teacher preparation, teaching practices, and student learning outcomes (Bier, Horn, Campbell, et al., 2012).

Purposeful collaboration is focused on what candidates and teachers need to know and be able to do to support student growth and development in all areas including academic, psychological, and social. Dialogue among teacher educators and partners focus on content knowledge and pedagogical content knowledge required for teaching specific subject matter, creating a supportive social context for learning, and developing relationships with and among students. Further, purposeful collaboration addresses issues related to school and district policies, practices, and student learning and developmental outcomes; and preservice teacher preparation policies, practices, outcomes, and impact. Shared understanding of goals, policies, and practices is an important outcome for purposeful collaboration. These discussions often reveal specific problems of practice that are of mutual concern and that can form the basis for joint activity producing interventions or solutions. Interventions and solutions for specific problems of practice provide a mutual benefit for teacher educators and practitioners, and advance knowledge for the profession when shared through publications in professional journals or at state and national conferences (see Chapter 2).

Assessment of Professional Knowledge and Skills

The assessment of professional knowledge and skills can be formative for the purpose of monitoring progress towards competent teaching such as key assessments, summative for the purpose of determining readiness for professional teaching practice such as state assessments for licensure, or to evaluate the continuous improvement of professional practice and learning outcomes for students.

Meaningful and productive formative assessments reinforce the epistemic practices incorporated into program courses and clinical experiences; and indicate candidates' progress in developing the expected habits of mind, professional knowledge, and teaching practices. Summative assessments measure candidates' ability to integrate and apply to practice deep knowledge of learners, learning, subject matter, and pedagogy; and to make appropriate assessments of progress towards achieving the expected learning and developmental outcomes for age, grade level, and subject matter for students in different contexts and with different developmental needs, cultural, linguistic, and experiential backgrounds.

The evaluation of teaching for the continuous improvement of professional practice and learning outcomes is focused on:

- the use of appropriate approaches for data gathering and analysis;
- the application of findings from data analysis to practice for correcting misunderstandings and perceptions that inhibit subsequent learning and progress in meeting learning and developmental expectations;
- identifying and correcting gaps in students' knowledge and skills; and
- supporting students in social and emotional development, including self-regulation for independent learning and self-discipline.

In this discussion, the term key assessment refers to specifically designed formative measures of progress towards mastery of expected professional knowledge and skills through a process that supports internalizing core habits of mind and professional practices. Key assessment goals and tasks are based on course objectives that directly link to state and national standards, research and theory, and identifiable and persistent problems of practice in the field that are foundational for competent teaching. In addition to measuring progress towards developing the expected knowledge and skills for competent teaching, epistemic practices such as focused inquiry, directed observation, and guided practice when embedded in a key assessment format that includes gathering data, analyzing data, and writing a commentary support habits of mind that reinforce the application of theory to practice and the continuous improvement of teaching.

An example of a goal for a key assessment is to measure candidates' progress in understanding instructional practices such as using small groups for specific learning tasks or supporting a socially isolated or excluded student. In this example, candidates demonstrate their knowledge of using small group instruction by conducting an observation that includes documenting the learning task, the social dynamic among group members, factors that influenced task completion, and the extent to which the task was completed. Candidates analyze and interpret the data and write a commentary that includes suggestions for improving the quality of learning and participation in the small group. Suggestions are based on academic knowledge connected to the assessment. In the case of the isolated or excluded student, candidates document the observable behavior of the student and the interaction with peers, use a recommended protocol for interviewing the student and the classroom teacher, analyze and interpret the data and write a commentary that includes an intervention plan for supporting the isolated student in making connections and building relationships with peers. The intervention plan is based on academic knowledge connected to the assessment. The tasks in key assessments are valid and reliable to the extent that they are consistently accurate in measuring candidates' progress in developing the expected professional knowledge or skills.

Usually, when candidates have satisfactorily completed all requirements for licensure, including academic and clinical experiences and passed all key assessments at the required proficiency level, they can be recommended for licensure. State licensure requirements often include a summative assessment designed to determine readiness for professional practice in classrooms. The edTPA is an example of a performance assessment available nationwide that is administered to preservice teachers to determine readiness for professional practice. The edTPA is a subject-specific performance assessment focused on measuring candidates' preparation for planning, instruction, and assessment of student learning. The edTPA assessment tasks are embedded in clinical practice and include a three to five-day documented learning segment. Supporting students in meeting the requirements of the edTPA has resulted in the faculty at some universities redesigning and aligning courses and clinical experiences for more effective teacher preparation (Lachuk & Koellner, 2015).

Formative assessments such as key assessments monitor progress towards teaching competence, performance assessments such as the edTPA measure readiness for professional practice, and inservice teaching evaluations are measures of progress towards accomplished teaching. Accomplished teaching is defined as expert practice applying deep knowledge of learners, learning, subject matter, pedagogy, and assessment of learning in designing meaningful and productive learning experiences and making adjustments in practices as needed to *consistently* enable all learners to meet the developmental expectations for their age, grade level, and subject matter. Candidates who have completed a well-designed program, with developmentally sequenced and interrelated academic and clinical experiences, and where progress was monitored through key assessments are well prepared to use a self-evaluation for attaining the level of accomplished teaching. The teaching practices inventory (Hollins, 2019) is an example of self-assessment that includes an examination of students' academic engagement, social interaction, psychological dispositions, and physical characteristics.

Programmatic Assessment

> New accountability reforms define effective teachers, at least in part, as those who produce higher student test score gains. In response, states are scrambling to create sophisticated databases that are able to link practicing teachers to their preparation programs as well as to the achievement data of the students they teach.
>
> *(Henry et al., 2012, p. 335)*

This statement represents a paradigm shift from the evaluation of components of teacher preparation programs and the qualification of faculty to outputs, including the performance of graduates as classroom teachers and their impact on P-12 student learning outcomes. The shift from inputs to outputs often conceals systemic challenges in program design and pedagogical practices in teacher preparation that are directly related to the classroom performance of program graduates and their impact on student learning outcomes. For example, many courses in teacher preparation programs are designed by individual faculty in isolation, based on personal judgment and preferences, disconnected from other courses and clinical experiences, and often taught at a time and place chosen by the instructor without regard for course sequencing. This situation indicates that attention to both inputs and outputs is required for improving teacher preparation and P-12 student learning outcomes. Such issues can be addressed in the program evaluation process.

In a discussion of the recent approaches to program evaluation, Hall, Smith, and Nowinski (2005) pointed out that: "Probably the most fundamental reason that program evaluations are limited is that there has not been a clear, consistent, and shared framework for organizing the many variables that comprise teacher education practice and relating these to evidence of effectiveness" (p. 20). These authors present a framework that shows the relationship among institutional mission, state and national standards, courses and clinical experiences (knowledge, skills, and dispositions), and accomplishments (candidate performance and impact). The results of the program evaluation are used for external reporting, program improvement, and candidate self-improvement. This approach to program evaluation differs significantly from that used in state and national accreditation of teacher preparation programs.

Presently, teacher preparation program evaluation is most often associated with state and national accreditation processes. For example, the Council for the Accreditation of Educator Preparation (CAEP) has five standards for judging the quality of educator preparation programs that include:

1. content and pedagogical knowledge;
2. clinical partnerships and practice;
3. candidate quality, recruitment, and selectivity;
4. program impact; and
5. provider quality assurance and continuous improvement.

Additionally, CAEP accredited educator preparation providers complete an annual report on eight measures that include:

1. impact on P-12 learning and development,
2. indicators of teaching effectiveness,
3. satisfaction of employers and employment milestones,
4. satisfaction of completers,
5. graduation rates,
6. ability of completers to meet licensing and any other state requirements,

7.   ability of completers to be hired in education positions for which they have prepared, and

8.   student loan default rates and other consumer information.

The CAEP standards and eight annual measures are important factors in monitoring the quality of teacher preparation programs; however, these practices have not yet had a noticeable impact on learning outcomes for the nation's school children.

State and national standards do not provide direct guidance for program improvement. However, the quality of the teacher preparation program influences the classroom performance of graduates and their impact on P-12 student learning outcomes. Candidates' preparation is supported by coherence, consistency, and continuity in the program design that provide access to professional knowledge and skills. Improving the preparation of candidates requires programmatic assessment that determines the conceptual and structural integrity of the teacher preparation program. Programmatic assessment requires the systematic collection and analysis of specific evidence. Program improvement requires application of the findings from data analysis.

Evidence of Conceptual Integrity

The documentation of consistent application across academic and clinical experiences of well-articulated statements of the philosophical stance, theoretical perspective for learning teaching, and epistemic practices for forming habits of mind provide evidence for coherence in program design. These conceptual elements of program design are evident in each course syllabus in resources (readings, videos, etc.), course assignments, and in-class learning experiences. These conceptual elements are evident in protocols for directed observations and guided practice in clinical experiences.

Evidence of continuity is an important factor in assessing program design. Continuity is present when it can be demonstrated that learning experiences and professional knowledge are interrelated, cumulative, increasing in complexity, and developmentally sequenced across courses and clinical experiences.

The documentation of consistency in professional knowledge and assignments included in courses over time, and in the application of protocols for clinical experiences is the final indicator of conceptual integrity in the program design. Internal consistency in the program design supports collecting reliable and valid data for program improvement.

Evidence of Program Structural Integrity

Structural integrity in a preservice program refers to the extent to which elements such as program admission practices, alignment across academic and clinical experiences, and the monitoring and assessment of professional knowledge and skills support program conceptual elements. For example, the philosophical stance and theoretical perspective should be evident in the practices and tools used in the selection and admission of candidates for the preservice program. Conceptual elements should be evident in the application materials submitted and questions asked during interviews of prospective candidates.

Evidence of program structural integrity is supported when it is documented that courses and clinical experiences are aligned to specific state and national standards that are developmentally sequenced. The standards have been translated to specific learning outcomes appropriate for the course content. The learning experiences and resource materials support learning outcomes. Each course includes at least one assignment that requires application to practice in an authentic school or community setting as appropriate. Academic knowledge and clinical experiences are interconnected, cumulative, and developmentally sequenced. The learning experiences within each course and clinical experience reflect the philosophical stance, theoretical perspective, and epistemic practices for the program.

Program structural integrity requires that monitoring and assessing professional knowledge and skills are consistent with the philosophical stance, theoretical perspective, and epistemic practices for the program. The philosophical stance indicates the expected outcomes and impact of the teacher preparation program. The monitoring and assessment practices are specifically designed to measure candidates' progress in developing the expected professional knowledge and skills. Monitoring and assessment are focused on appropriate translation and application of professional knowledge to practice. Valid monitoring and assessment instruments are based on the standards and learning outcomes included in academic and clinical experiences. Procedures for monitoring candidates' progress have well-designed protocols, standards for scoring, scores are independent of grades in courses, measure knowledge and skills developed across more than one course or clinical experience, and scores are consequential in advancement towards program completion. Approaches to monitoring candidates' progress are reliable to the extent that they consistently provide accurate information regarding what candidates know and can do.

Conclusion

In the final analysis, the trustworthiness of a preservice teacher preparation program is determined by its consistency in preparing teachers whose students regularly meet the expectations for their age, grade level, and subject matter areas. The probability for attaining a high level of trustworthiness is influenced by the extent to which the program is characterized by coherence, continuity, and consistency. Advancement of the teaching profession is influenced by the extent that research is conducted on programs characterized by coherence, continuity, and consistency. Otherwise, it is difficult to understand what is being investigated, how data should be analyzed, how findings should be interpreted and applied for the improvement of practice.

References

American Association of Colleges for Teacher Education (AACTE) Clinical Practice Commission (2018). *A pivot toward clinical practice, its lexicon, and the renewal of educator preparation.* Washington, DC: AACTE.

Aragon, A., Culpepper, S. A., McKee, M. W., & Perkins, M. (2014). Understanding the profiles of preservice teachers with different levels of commitment to teaching in urban schools. *Urban Education*, 49 (5), 543–573.

Ball, D. L. & Forzani, F. M. (2009). The work of teaching and the challenge of teacher education. *Journal of Teacher Education*, 60 (5), 497–511.

Ball, D. L. & Forzani, F. M. (2010). Teaching skillful teaching. *Educational Leadership*, 68 (4), 40–45.

Ball, D. L., Sleep, L., Boerst, T. A., & Bass, H. (2009). Combining the development of practice and the practice of development in teacher education. *The Elementary School Journal*, 109, 458–474.

Bier, M. L., Horn, I., Campbell, S. S., Kazemi, E., Hintz, A., Kelley-Petersen, M., Stevens, R., Saxena, A., & Peck, C. (2012). Designs for simultaneous renewal in university-public school partnerships: Hitting the "sweet spot". *Teacher Education Quarterly*, 39 (3), 127–141.

Burrough, G., Lewis, A., Battery, D., Curran, M., Hyland, N. E., & Ryan, S. (2020). From mediated fieldwork to co-constructed partnerships: A framework for guiding and reflecting P-12 school-university partnerships. *Journal of Teacher Education*, 71 (1), 122–134.

Caskey, M. M., Peterson, K. D., & Temple, J. B. (2001). Complex admission selection procedures for a graduate preservice teacher education program. *Teacher Education Quarterly*, 28 (4), 7–21.

Darling-Hammond, L. (2006). Constructing 21st century teacher education. *Journal of Teacher Education*, 57 (3), 300–314.

Falkenberg, T. (June 22, 2010). Admission to teacher education programs: The problem and two approaches to addressing it. *Canadian Journal of Educational Administration and Policy*, 107, 1–35.

Grossman, P., Compton, C., Igra, D., Ronfeldt, M., Shahan, E., & Williamson, P. W. (2009). Teaching practice: A cross-professional perspective. *Teachers College Record*, 111 (9), 2055–2100.

Hall, G. E., Smith, C., & Nowinski, M. B. (2005). An organizing framework for using evidence-based assessments to improve teaching and learning in teacher education programs. *Teacher Education Quarterly*, 32 (3), 19–33.

Henry, G. T., Kershaw, D. C., Zulli, R. A., & Smith, A. A. (2012). Incorporating teacher effectiveness into teacher preparation program evaluation. *Journal of Teacher Education*, 63 (5), 335–355.

Hollins, E. R. (2011). Teacher preparation for quality teaching. *Journal of Teacher Education*, 62 (4), 395–407.

Hollins, E. R. (2019). *Teaching to transform urban schools and communities: Powerful pedagogy in practice.* New York: Routledge.

Kumar, M. (2006). Constructivist epistemology in action. *The Journal of Educational Thought*, 40 (3), 247–261.

Lachuk, A. J. & Koellner, K. (2015). Performance-based assessment for certification: Insights from edTPA implementation. *Language Arts*, 93 (2), 84–95.

Levin, J. R. (1986). Four cognitive principles of learning-strategy instruction. *Educational Psychologist*, 21 (1 & 2), 3–17.

Mayer, R. F. (2001). What good is educational psychology? The case of cognition and instruction. *Educational Psychologist*, 36 (2), 83–88.

McDiarmid, G. W. & Caprino, K. (2018). *Lessons from the Teachers for a New Era Project: Evidence and accountability in teacher education*. New York: Routledge.

McDonald, M., Kazemi, E., & Kavanaugh, S. S. (2013). Core practices and pedagogies of teacher education: A call for a common language and collective activity. *Journal of Teacher Education*, 64 (5), 378–386.

National Council for Accreditation of Teacher Education (NCATE) Blue Ribbon Panel on Clinical Preparation for Improved Student Learning. (2010). *Transforming teacher education through clinical practice: A national strategy to prepare effective teachers*. Washington, DC: NCATE.

Partelow, L. (2019). *What to make of declining enrollment in teacher preparation programs*. Washington, DC: Center for American Progress. www.americanprogress.org/issues/education-k-12/reports/2019/12/03/477311/make-declining-enrollment-teacher-preparation-programs/.

Piaget, J. (1953). *The origin of intelligence in the child*. New York: Routledge and Kegan Paul.

Schmid, R. (2018). Pockets of excellence: Teacher beliefs and behaviors that lead to high student achievement at low achieving schools. *Sage Open*, July-September, 1–10. doi:10.1177/2158244018797238.

Shiveley, J. & Misco, T. (2010). "But how do I know about their attitudes and beliefs?": A four-step process for integrating and assessing dispositions in teacher education. *The Clearing House*, 83 (1), 9–14.

Teachers for a New Era: A national initiative to improve the quality of teaching. (2001). New York: Carnegie Corporation of New York.

Thompson, J., Hagenah, S., Lohwasser, K., & Laxton, K. (2015). Problems without ceilings: How mentors and novices frame and work on problems-of-practice. *Journal of Teacher Education*, 66 (4), 363–381.

Torrez, C. A. & Krebs, M. (2020). *The teacher residency model: Core components for high impact on student achievement*. New York: Lexington Books.

Vygotsky, L. S. (1978). *Thought and language*. Cambridge, MA: MIT Press.

Yilmaz, K. (2011). The cognitive perspective on learning: Its theoretical underpinnings and implications for classroom practices. *The Clearing House*, 84 (5), 204–212.

Yilmaz, K. (2008). Constructivism: Its theoretical underpinnings, variations, and implications for classroom instruction. *Educational Horizons*, 86 (3), 161–172.

4

PROGRAM EXPLICATION

Introduction

Chapter 1 in this volume defines academically based teacher preparation as a meticulously designed approach grounded in the most reliable research, theory, and practice available; and that employs continuous data gathering and analysis for validation and improvement of practices, outcomes, and impact. Academically based teacher preparation has central characteristics of coherence, continuity, consistency, and trustworthiness. Instrumental characteristics of academically based teacher preparation include collaboration among stakeholders, interrelatedness among conceptual and structural elements, and systematic data collection. Chapter 3 articulates a framework for teacher preparation program design that includes the conceptual elements of philosophical stance, theoretical perspective on learning to teach, professional knowledge and skills, epistemic practices, and structural elements such as admission practices, alignment of courses and clinical experiences, school partnerships, assessment of professional knowledge and skills, and program evaluation. In academically based teacher preparation, these conceptual and structural elements are integrally connected and mutually supportive.

This chapter delineates a program explication process that supports both the central and instrumental characteristics of academically based teacher preparation and facilitates the connection between conceptual and structural elements. The program explication process provides a statement about what teachers at a specific level and content area need to know and be able to do to meet the needs of students and is grounded in the philosophical stance and theoretical perspective on learning to teach for the program. In the described process, faculty make deliberate comparisons of new and existing program requirements to determine the need for adjustments in courses and learning experiences. This approach adds transparency to curriculum development and cultivates shared understanding and ownership among faculty. The process delineated in this chapter addresses persistent problems of practice in teacher preparation that include the instability of the professional knowledge base due to individual faculty ownership of courses and programs, organizational fragmentation, and lack of program transparency.

Addressing Problems of Practice

One of the first calls in the United States for systematic teacher education came from Horace Mann, a founder of the common school movement, who critiqued the limited knowledge and skill of the teaching force (Bergen, 1992). The proliferation of common schools in the 19th century increased the demand for more teachers and improvement in the quality of teaching. This resulted in the development of normal schools intended to train professional teachers in systematic ways. Early normal schools tended to be connected to local common schools and were controlled by local school boards. As these smaller institutions gave way to state-sponsored normal schools, additional levels of bureaucracy brought new voices and new critiques to the field of teacher education.

By the 1960s, normal schools had evolved from state teachers' colleges into regional public universities, and university schools or departments of education had become the primary providers of teacher preparation in the United States (Labaree, 2008). Universities dominated the delivery of teacher preparation through the end of the 20th century (Fraser, 2007). However, in response to criticism that started as preparation moved into the university and has persisted (Bestor, 1953; Conant, 1963; Koerner, 1963), alternatives to traditional university-based teacher preparation have gained acceptance and recognition (Cochran-Smith et al., 2020; Zeichner & Bier, 2015). These alternative teacher preparation programs have served many different purposes including attempts at teacher preparation reform motivated in part by persistent problems of practice such as program fragmentation, the instability in the professional knowledge base, the composition of the teaching force, and the failure to improve student learning outcomes in P-12 schools.

Program Fragmentation

There are multiple sources of fragmentation in teacher preparation programs including factors that are conceptual, structural, and organizational. Conceptual and structural elements in program design are discussed in Chapter 3. However, it is important to point out that conceptual fragmentation results from inadequate development and articulation of the philosophical stance, theoretical perspective, professional knowledge base, and epistemic practices. The philosophical stance and theoretical perspective are foundational in framing the professional knowledge base and epistemic practices. The knowledge base and epistemic practices are at the core for learning the theory, research, practices, and routines for teaching. Disruption or fragmentation among these conceptual elements negatively impacts the development of teaching competence and P-12 student learning outcomes. Among the most common sources of conceptual fragmentation is faculty owning courses and making independent adjustments in course content that cause instability in the program knowledge base (Flores, 2016; Lanier & Little, 1986; Tom, 1997).

Structural fragmentation occurs when the conceptual and structural elements are not consistently interrelated, and structural elements are not well developed and articulated. The knowledge base and epistemic practices (conceptual elements) directly influence what candidates learn in the application of academic knowledge to practice during clinical experiences and the evidence of progress in developing teaching competence as measured in assessments of professional knowledge and skills (structural element). Instability in the knowledge base influences the quality of learning during clinical experiences.

Organizational fragmentation refers to displacements, disruptions, inconsistencies, and irregularities in the unit or institutional systems, policies, and practices that form the context for teacher preparation. The contextual conditions for teacher preparation programs impact the articulation and interrelationship among conceptual and structural elements. For example, the underfunding and inadequate staffing of teacher preparation programs that result in dependence on adjuncts for teaching courses and retired practitioners for supervising clinical experiences often contribute to instability in the professional knowledge base and disrupt the application of academic knowledge to practice process.

The discussion in this chapter is focused on a program explication process that mitigates some effects of organizational fragmentation by increasing coherence and consistency in the professional knowledge base for teacher preparation. The program explication process makes the professional knowledge base fully transparent and systematically aligned with standards set by state and national accrediting agencies, professional organizations, and regional institutional accrediting agencies and knowledge from research, theory, and practice. The program explication process is part of the preparation for program authorization, approval, and accreditation.

Program Authorization, Approval, and Accreditation

Program authorization, approval, and accreditation present significant challenges for many program providers. Among the most intractable challenges are those related to budgetary and other resources, including expertise and time for completing the work of program renewal, approval, and accreditation. Not all teacher educators are knowledgeable about the literature on learning to teach, curriculum development, a framework for teaching, or the program approval and accreditation process (Pinnegar, 2005; Thornton, 2001). Yet, teacher educators are responsible for the knowledge base for teaching and teacher preparation. Teacher educators serving as tenured or tenure track faculty at universities have full time responsibilities that include teaching, scholarship, and service. Allocating significant amounts of time for participating in program renewal and accreditation can disrupt scholarship efforts and delay the promotion and tenure process.

Respect for teacher educators' time and expertise requires a well-organized approach that includes protocols, tools, and a timeline that increase efficiency and effectiveness and make the process of program design and renewal meaningful and productive. The timeline assists teacher educators in managing their own time and ensures that all deadlines are met. Figure 4.1 illustrates the process of approval and authorization for program changes. Table 4.1 is an example of a timeline indicating when specific evidence for compliance is to be completed. The program explication process in this chapter and the course alignment process in Chapter 5 support teacher educators' collaboration and participation in program development and renewal.

The Program Explication Process

The approach presented in this discussion is an example of a program explication process that has been successfully implemented. However, teacher preparation programs are in different contexts and serve different purposes and populations. Throughout this chapter, the word *course* is used to delineate a specific format for delivering professional knowledge for candidates in a preservice teacher preparation program. This is the primary format used in university-based teacher preparation. However, some program providers prefer a modular format rather than the traditional course format. The modular format has greater flexibility and efficiency for reconfiguration when accommodating different licensure areas in the same teacher preparation program. For example, a general methods module

All new proposals for courses and programs and modifications of existing courses and programs follow policies and procedures for approval by the unit faculty and institution. Subsequently, programs are submitted for approval at the state, regional, and national levels.

FIGURE 4.1 Program approval process

TABLE 4.1 Program approval process schedule

Program approval process schedule	Due date
Program explication documents provided for teacher preparation faculty review	9/1/2021
Approval of program explication documents by teacher preparation faculty	10/1/2021
Faculty approve changes to degree/certification programs	11/1/2021
Institutional approval for changes to degree/certification programs	12/1/2021
Institutionally approved degree/certificate programs submitted for state and regional approval (e.g., Higher Learning Commission)	2/1/2021
Full implementation of approved programs	9/1/2022
Submit approved programs for national accreditation (e.g., CAEP)	9/1/2023

Institutional deadlines for course and program approval, and state and national deadlines for program approval and accreditation are fixed. Agency approval is required for modification.

used across licensure areas can be linked to discipline specific modules as appropriate for middle, secondary, or other single subject licensure areas. The explication process and its associated documents can be adapted to meet specific needs and a variety of formats.

The explication process is intended to make the knowledge base for teacher preparation programs coherent and transparent, fully engage stakeholders in the program design process, ensure that programs meet state and national standards for accreditation, and to serve the interest of the teaching profession and the nation's children by preparing competent teachers. It promotes continuity in the preservice teacher preparation program by enabling developmental sequencing of methodically aligned professional knowledge and clinical experiences to foster learning that is interrelated, increasingly complex, and cumulative.

Determining What Constitutes a Program

There are several ways to define a teacher preparation program. A program can be defined as a single licensure area with conceptual and structural elements or as a unit with several licensure areas linked to the same conceptual and structural elements. In the first definition, each licensure area is a program that requires a separate explication process. In the second definition, there is one explication process for the program with a separate analysis for the unique aspects of each licensure area. It is reasonable to use a separate explication process for each licensure area in both definitions.

In the explication process detailed in this chapter, what constitutes a program was determined by internal institutional factors such as specific degrees associated with licensure, and by external mandates that influence conceptual or structural elements in program design, such as state regulations that set standards for admission and completion in areas of licensure. The explication process was completed for each licensure area at both the graduate and undergraduate level. The central purpose for the explication process was to develop the transparency necessary for faculty and stakeholder collaboration resulting in program quality indicators of coherence, continuity, and consistency; and faculty participation leading to shared ownership of all aspects of teacher preparation.

Leading Program Explication

As discussed in Chapter 2, teacher preparation program design is a collaborative endeavor. In this approach, faculty leadership is especially important. Lead faculty members were identified for each licensure area based on expertise and experience with the subject matter and licensure requirements. For example, the coordinator for secondary English education licensure was identified as lead faculty member for the explication process for the secondary English program. This colleague was a member of the English Language Arts Teacher Educators (ELATE) group of the National Council of Teachers of English (NCTE), an instructor of English Language Arts methods courses, and a former secondary English teacher. A lead faculty member assumes responsibility for completing a draft explication for each program. In cases where a faculty member with the knowledge and experience necessary for deep engagement with a particular program is not available, the unit can employ an expert to design the program and have it vetted or peer reviewed by other experts in the field. In some institutions, program and course peer review are common practices that contribute to program trustworthiness.

Articulating Program Focus

The preliminary preparation for the explication process is articulating the program focus. In addition to the grade level and subject matter requirements, each licensure area requires a clearly articulated focus that is aligned with the conceptual and structural elements of the teacher preparation program. The program focus will be evident in descriptions of the licensure requirements, course titles, and course descriptions. Chapter 3 includes a description of the Percy Julian Science Teacher Preparation program that models an articulation approach that can be applied to a single licensure area prior to the explication process.

Articulating a focus contextualizes and frames the interpretation and application of state and national standards and other program requirements. For example, the philosophical stance or purpose for a licensure area influences the professional knowledge base and clinical experiences. The individual courses or modules that constitute the knowledge base reflect the philosophical stance. Meeting the demands of the philosophical stance may require additions to the knowledge base not mandated by state and national accreditation agencies.

Identifying Source Documents

There are at least five institutions or agencies that reposit documents involving policies, procedures, standards, and regulations that influence teacher preparation program design and renewal. The repositories for these documents include the local university or other program provider, regional accreditation agencies for higher education, state accreditation agencies, national accreditation agencies, and professional organizations. Information on existing and previously approved teacher preparation programs and licensure areas are on file at the local university or other program provider, the appropriate unit at the state department of education, and the regional accreditation agency for higher education. Any degree, program, or licensure area not listed as approved or authorized at one or more of these levels requires corrective action. Correcting this situation requires guidance from the university administration or the administrator for the program provider. There are potentially severe consequences for offering unauthorized programs or programs that have not been appropriately approved.

The program approval and authorization documents for existing teacher preparation programs indicate the courses, clinical experiences, and other conditions for program implementation that were required at the time. Significant changes in an authorized program require approval from the state accreditation agency and the regional accrediting agency for higher education.

Each faculty lead is expected to collect and review the appropriate source documents (Table 4.2) and develop a timeline (Table 4.1) for meeting the requirements for each agency involved in the program approval process. These source documents are used in conjunction with the program explication document to complete this aspect of program development or renewal.

The InTASC standards (CCSO, 2016) provide a developmental sequence and progression that can be used in new programs for organizing a matrix that includes state standards, other requirements, and mandates that facilitates the program explication process. This matrix is useful in developing the knowledge base for teacher preparation, developing course descriptions, and in sequencing courses or modules.

Understanding the Explication Document

The explication process is supported by a program explication document. This document is composed of four sections. The first section, *Program Information and Context*, identifies the specific degree or licensure program, presents the primary focus, and clearly delineates requirements such as standards from state or national accreditation, professional organizations, and institutional assessments required for program authorization.

TABLE 4.2 Source documents for program explication

✓	Source documents for program explication
	Institutional documents
	Guidelines, policies, and procedures for program and course approval
	Published certificate/degree requirements (university catalog, website)
	Published course descriptions (university catalogue, website)
	Learning outcomes and expectations (Course syllabi)
	Institutional Assessment Reports
	Professional organizations
	Discipline specific or developmental standards for professional preparation
	Specialized Professional Association (SPA) reports
	State documents
	State certificate and licensure policies, regulations, and standards (existing and new)
	Certificates/programs previously approved or authorized by the state (state website)
	Report from previous state program approval/review
	Regional program approval documents
	Certificates/programs previously approved by regional higher education accreditor
	Reports from previous regional institutional review related to teacher preparation
	National accreditation documents
	Handbook of guidelines, policies, requirements, and standards
	Annual reports and data submitted
	Previous self-study report
	Report from previous accreditation review

Analysis of data from previous assessments, reports, and program reviews for approval and accreditation can reveal issues that need to be addressed in the program renewal process.

The second section, *Analysis of Existing Program,* presents an initial draft of program content or, in the case of redesign, it lists the existing content of the program. Courses shared across licensure programs and those provided by academic units outside of teacher education are clearly identified.

The third section, *Recommended Program Revisions,* indicates the courses within the program that need revision in response to state or national mandates, those that are not required, existing courses that meet newly identified needs, and new content or courses that are needed. Recommended changes require a detailed rationale linked to program purpose, standards, or institutional assessments.

In addition to these three sections, the program explication document is accompanied by a *Recommended Course Sequence,* providing a map of the developmental sequencing of courses in the program. Figure 4.2 shows a sample excerpt of a preliminary sequencing of courses based on the InTASC standards. A more refined developmental sequencing and alignment of courses is discussed in Chapter 5 in this book. An abridged sample explication document is provided in Appendix A of this chapter.

Analyzing Licensure and Accreditation Requirements

The impetus for developing a new teacher preparation program can be a response to local needs or shortages in the field, the development of models of practice for teaching or teacher preparation, or to address persistent problems of practice in the field. The emphasis for program renewal is most often in response to changes in state regulations, national mandates, a decline in enrollment or local competition. Regardless of the impetus, the program explication process requires a careful analysis of traditional approaches in constructing the knowledge base and other practices in teacher preparation, evidence from classroom and school practices indicating the need for changes in teacher preparation, and new state regulations and national mandates.

Redesigning an existing program in response to new state regulations, national mandates, and new evidence from practice requires a contrastive analysis of the existing and new requirements. This analysis includes a comparison of both structural elements that impact program admission and completion such as changes in credit requirements or clinical experience hours and conceptual elements such as changes in the knowledge base. Such changes are recorded in Section 1 of

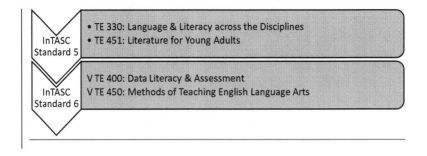

Program course sequence is linked to the developmental sequence of InTASC standards.

FIGURE 4.2 Sample preliminary course sequencing

the explication document. In the sample explication document provided in Appendix A, contrastive analysis of existing (2008) and new (2014) teacher education regulations for secondary English education in the State of Missouri revealed structural changes in required clinical hours and the number of credits required in literacy. Changes in the number of credit hours in literacy has an impact on the knowledge base as does the addition of *Knowledge of Individual Student Needs* and *Content Planning and Delivery*. When program redesign is prompted by changes in licensure regulations, as they are in the sample provided, all mandated changes are recorded in the explication document and appropriately labeled. The matrix described earlier supports the explication process for new programs.

The failure to fully address and comply with all state requirements can result in delays or denial of program authorization or approval. Offering a teacher licensure program that is not authorized or approved at the state level can have severe legal and financial consequences for candidates, faculty, and the university or other program providers.

Analyzing and Developing the Knowledge Base

Developing the knowledge base for teaching and teacher preparation is a high-stake endeavor that places teacher educators in the role of *architects for the teaching profession*. This process requires collaboration among teacher educators, arts and sciences faculty, school practitioners, community agencies, and other stakeholders. The matrix based on InTASC standards described earlier provides a source of information for conversations among stakeholders.

InTASC standards and progressions do not constitute a professional knowledge base or a basic framework for teaching and teacher preparation. Developing a knowledge base for a new program requires knowledge of the big ideas and concepts that form the *basic framework*. These big ideas include learners, learning, pedagogy, subject matter, and context (Figure 4.2). Understanding the interrelationship among

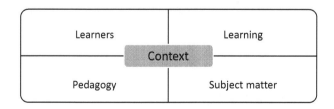

Context is the *gravitational field* and the *gravitational force* for teaching and learning.

FIGURE 4.3 Basic knowledge base framework for teaching

these ideas supports developing a knowledge base characterized by coherence, continuity, consistency, and purposeful redundancy. Context is the central organizing idea in a basic framework for the professional knowledge base. Learners are socialized, grow, and develop in a specific context. Theories of learning explain the learning process, the condition and context necessary for optimal learning. Pedagogy that produces meaningful and productive learning is responsive to the context in which learners have been socialized and the social context and social arrangements that best support learners from diverse cultural and experiential backgrounds. Subject matter is more accessible when it is contextualized within what learners know, have experienced, and value. In essence, *context* is the *gravitational field* and the *gravitational force* in teaching and learning. The power of *context* in teaching, learning, and learning to teach cannot be overstated. This *basic framework* clarifies the relationship among the big ideas in teaching and learning and provides guidance for using the InTASC and other standards.

Each licensure area includes both common and discipline specific aspects of the knowledge base for teaching and clinical experiences for the application of knowledge to practice. The explication process engages faculty in analyzing the knowledge, skills, and experiences in each existing licensure area as compared to the new requirements and evidence from practice. This process is at the program level rather than the course or module level. The explication process makes the general contours of the knowledge base transparent. The course alignment process discussed in the Chapter 5 reveals the details of the knowledge base at the course or module level that allows for more refined analysis to ensure coherence, continuity, and consistency across courses and clinical experiences.

The second section on the explication document requires faculty to think holistically about course content in deciding where a course is to be listed. This means thinking about the five or six big ideas in the course and determining if the course description and title are appropriate. The course description and title should reflect the big ideas. Misalignment in the course description, title, and big ideas requires correction. In some instances, changing course descriptions and titles is considered significant enough to require review and approval through the appropriate university curriculum process. Courses are listed on the explication document based on the big ideas reflected in the language used in the course description and title.

Adjusting the Knowledge Base

Adjusting the professional knowledge base during program renewal for the purpose of meeting new standards and requirements is a complex process that has potential benefits and risks. The intended benefit is that of improving teaching practices, teacher preparation, and P-12 student learning. The potential risk is that this goal will not be achieved. The potential benefits and risks increase the value of evidence from the field in adjusting the knowledge base and clinical experiences. Each new standard or requirement is based on specific evidence from the field. For example, an increase in the number of credit hours required for literacy is based on data revealing low academic performance in reading in P-12 schools and for entering college freshmen. The new literacy course is intended to address specific issues identified by teacher educators and practitioners for improving student learning and performance. The competencies and standards are not intended as the knowledge base; but are to be included as important touchstones in the knowledge base.

Adjusting the professional knowledge base to accommodate new standards and regulations demands careful examination and deep thought. Several important questions need to be answered. What is the evidence supporting this change? What is the intended effect? What is the best approach for addressing the underlying issues? Thinking of each course as consisting of four or five modules each representing a big idea related to the framework for the knowledge base creates transparency at the course level and facilitates adjustments and corrections (see Chapter 5 for a discussion of aligning modules within courses). Addressing a standard or regulation can require reframing a module within a course, adding, or replacing a module. In some instances, new mandates focus attention on highly consequential and persistent issues or problems in the knowledge base such as that in literacy. The urgency in addressing this issue is indicated by the demand for additional time in the form of credit hours, which usually means adding a course or module. The central questions for teacher educators and stakeholders related to this demand are: What more do candidates need to know and be able to do to better facilitate literacy acquisition and development? What clinical experiences might facilitate the application of this knowledge to practice? What evidence might candidates produce to demonstrate understanding and the ability to apply knowledge to practice in literacy acquisition and development? What evidence from practice in the field might reveal the impact of this adjustment to the knowledge base?

The number of credit hours in a degree, teacher licensure program, or licensure area is usually regulated by the university, program provider, or the state department of education. Exceeding the limit on credit hours may require special approval. In cases where mandates include directives for adding credit hours without increasing the maximum number of credit hours allowed for a program means removing courses to avoid exceeding the limit. Removing a course is a serious adjustment to the knowledge base with potential consequences for professional practice. Questions that need to be addressed when removing a course include: How do the big ideas in this course inform teaching practices? What might be the impact of removing these big ideas? Can these big ideas be incorporated as modules in other courses? What evidence from practice will indicate the impact for removing specific big ideas from the knowledge base? The answers to these questions determine the action that will be taken.

In the final analysis, meeting all standards and regulations is required for program approval and authorization. This is not optional. Providing the best possible preparation for candidates and optimal education for P-12 students is the impetus for all standards and regulations. The quality of life in the society depends on the preparation of teachers for providing optimal education for the nation's children and youth.

Investigating Adjustments in the Knowledge Base

New mandates, standards, and regulations are invitations for collaborative longitudinal research projects focused on improving teaching, teacher preparation, and learning outcomes for P-12 students. Many factors influence the response to mandates and regulations, including teacher educators' interpretation of meaning and intent, expertise, perspectives, values, and resources available. These are high stakes decisions that significantly impact candidates, P-12 students, local communities, and the nation made by teacher educators in assuming the role of *architects for the teaching profession*. Ethical standards from several professional organizations including the National Education Association and the National Association for the Education of Young Children require that teachers and teacher educators demonstrate commitment to the highest standards of professional practice and responsibility, and continuously strive to improve practice in the profession. An important responsibility for teacher educators is developing and maintaining a trustworthy knowledge base for teaching and teacher preparation. Determining trustworthiness for the knowledge base requires research.

Research related to the application to practice of academic knowledge influenced by new mandates and regulations is especially important. For example, when responding to a mandate that requires increasing credit hours in literacy, teacher educators carefully select from research, theory, and practice those big ideas directly related to the problem in teaching practice addressed by the mandate. The research investigates questions about the appropriateness and impact on candidates' understanding, ability to apply the new knowledge to practice, and the impact on P-12 student learning. The findings from this research informs the improvement of the knowledge base and practices in the teacher preparation program for which the data were gathered and analyzed.

Research on new mandates and regulations serves multiple purposes beyond improving the local teacher preparation program. Well designed and published research studies inform the field on what is effective and what is not, under what conditions, and for whom. Such research studies include a description of the mandate, the problem the mandate is intended to address, the program change or intervention responding to the mandate, data collection and findings. Research studies on mandates and regulations inform policy makers, accreditation agencies, and school practitioners. Policy makers and accreditation agencies better understand how teacher educators interpret and respond to mandates, standards, and regulations. This can serve to improve directives for the field. This research better informs school practitioners on how to understand and make use of research on teaching and teacher preparation, and what information is important to share when collaborating with teacher educators.

Finally, research in the context of a well-designed teacher preparation program that includes a well-articulated and stable knowledge base, meticulously aligned courses and clinical experiences has potential for validating the knowledge base and identifying trustworthy practices for teaching and teacher preparation. The sources of data from this type of practice-based research includes that from regular practices and routines such as the observation of advanced clinical experiences (teaching) using pre- and post-observation protocols and observation checklists, candidates' notes and commentaries from clinical experiences, and key assessments (see Chapter 7 for a detailed discussion of key assessments). Practice-based research conducted within the context of an academically based and well-designed preservice teacher preparation program could set new standards for research and practice that increase trustworthiness and the predictability for effectiveness in classroom teaching and student learning outcomes.

Conclusion

This chapter describes a program explication process that supports both the central and instrumental characteristics of academically based teacher preparation and facilitates the connection between conceptual and structural elements. This process addresses persistent problems of practice in teacher preparation that include program fragmentation and program approval and accreditation. The explication process supports the development, analysis, adjustment, and research on the effectiveness of the knowledge base for teaching and teacher preparation. The Program Explication Document facilitates faculty collaboration and shared ownership in the program design, approval, and accreditation process.

References

Bergen, T. J. (1992). The criticisms of teacher education: A historical perspective. *Teacher Education Quarterly*, 19 (2), 5–18.

Bestor, A. E. (1953). *Educational wastelands: The retreat from learning in our public schools*. Champaign, IL: University of Illinois Press.

Cochran-Smith, M., Keefe, E. S., Carney, M. C., Sánchez, J. G., Olivo, M., & Smith, R. J. (2020). Teacher preparation at new graduate schools of education: Studying a controversial innovation. *Teacher Education Quarterly*, 47 (2), 8–37.

Conant, J. B. (1963). *The education of American teachers*. New York, NY: McGraw-Hill.

Council of Chief State School Officers (CCSO) (2016). *Interstate teacher assessment and support consortium*. (InTASC). http://programs.ccsso.org/projects/interstate_new_teacher_assessment_and_support_consortium/.

Flores, M. A. (2016). Teacher education curriculum. In J. Loughran & M. L. Hamilton (Eds.), *International handbook of teacher education*, vol. 1 (pp. 187–230). Singapore: Springer.

Fraser, J. W. (2007). *Preparing America's teachers: A history.* New York, NY: Teachers College Press.

Koerner, J. D. (1963). *The miseducation of American teachers.* Boston, MA: Houghton Mifflin.

Labaree, D. F. (2008). An uneasy relationship: The history of teacher education in the university. In M. Cochran-Smith, S. Feiman-Nemser, D. J. McIntyre, & K. E. Demers (Eds.), *Handbook of research on teacher education: Enduring questions in changing contexts.* (3rd ed., pp. 290–306). New York, NY: Routledge.

Lanier, J. & Little, J. W. (1986). Research in teacher education. In M. C. Wittrock (Ed.), *Handbook of research on teaching.* (3rd ed., pp. 527–560). New York, NY: MacMillan.

Missouri Department of Elementary and Secondary Education (2008, January). *Certification requirements for secondary education (Grades 9–12).* Jefferson City, MO: Author.

Pinnegar, S. (2005). Identity development, moral authority and the teacher educator. In G. F. Hoban (Ed.), *The missing links in teacher education design.* (pp. 259–279). Dordrecht, Netherlands: Springer.

Rules of the Department of Elementary and Secondary Education. (2014). *Missouri Code of State Regulations,* 5 CSR 20–400.

Thornton, S. J. (2001). Educating the educators: Rethinking subject matter and methods. *Theory into Practice,* 40 (1), 72–78.

Tom, A. (1997). *Redesigning teacher education.* Albany, NY: SUNY Press.

Zeichner, K. & Bier, M. (2015). Opportunities and pitfalls in the turn toward clinical experience in U.S. teacher education. In E. R. Hollins (Ed.), *Rethinking field experiences in preservice teacher preparation: Meeting new challenges for accountability.* (pp. 20–46). New York: Routledge.

Appendix A: Program Explication Document (Abridged)

Section 1: Program Information and Context

Program: Bachelor of Arts in Secondary Education, English 9–12
Program Focus: To prepare students for state certification to teach English Language Arts for grades 9–12, with a particular emphasis on preparation to teach in urban schools and meeting the needs of learners from diverse backgrounds.

Mandated Program Changes (State or National):

1. Literacy coursework required for all secondary certifications increased from three credits[1] to six credits[2]

2. Differentiated Learning, Classroom Management, and Cultural Diversity now listed as core competencies for knowledge of Individual Student Needs[2]

3. Assessment, Student Data, and Data-based Decision-Making; Critical Thinking and Problem Solving; and English Language Learning now listed as core competencies for Content Planning and Delivery[2]

Section 2: Analysis of Existing Program

TABLE A1 Content of existing program

Professional knowledge and skills	Existing course covering whole or large part of framework component	Learning outcomes specifically targeting framework component
Learner development	TE 300	Teacher candidate will identify developmental and learning characteristics of students as they relate to physical, cognitive, moral, identity and social development.
	TE 302	Teacher candidate will engage in critical thinking and reflective decision making regarding educational issues related to child development
Learning environments	TE 303	No outcomes listed/no assessments directly related

Current Shared Coursework:

Shared with all Middle and Secondary Certification Areas

TE 300: Educational Psychology (three credits)
TE 302: Adolescent Development (three credits)

Current Courses Delivered by other Academic Units

Delivered by Department of Educational Psychology

TE 300: Educational Psychology (three credits)
TE 302: Adolescent Development (three credits)

Section 3: Recommended Program Revisions

Revised/Renamed Courses:

TE 303: Analyzing Learning Environments in Urban Contexts (three credits) *(formerly Classroom Teaching)*

> *Description of and Rationale for Revision:* Past syllabi for TE 303 vary widely, and very few of them match the course description in the catalogue. That course description is a mix of foundations, advising, and introductory field

experience, all of which are covered in more depth in other courses. Recommend revising this course to serve as the major vehicle for synthesizing and applying the content covered in the other courses in Block 1 and articulating a programmatic construction of classroom management as establishing productive learning environments, facilitating social interaction, and planning relevant and engaging learning experiences based upon deep knowledge of individual students' contexts and cultures.

TE 490: Capstone for Secondary Education (three credits)

Description of and Rationale for Revision: Currently TE 490 is a two-credit course; recommend upping to 3 credits and making it the course primarily responsible for meeting requirement for new required competency in Consultation and Collaboration, since candidates will have the best opportunity to apply the professional knowledge base on consultation and collaboration during their student teaching semester.

Pre-Existing Courses Added:

ENG 321: Sociolinguistics (3 credits)

Rationale for Add: State requirements for certification include coursework in modern English grammar. However, research indicates that teacher adherence to prescriptive views of grammar and correcting of perceived "errors" contributes to lower self-efficacy and academic achievement of students from diverse cultural and linguistic backgrounds. If candidates are to avoid these destructive views and practices, they will need a depth of knowledge in the social construction of language and an understanding of descriptive grammars.

Two courses (six credits) focused on the study of literature of underrepresented groups

Rationale for Add: Replacing two of the four current unrestricted electives with a curated list of electives focusing on the study of literature of underrepresented groups will ensure that ELA teacher candidates receive subject matter preparation that will align with partner district curricula and with the experiences and identities of P-12 students in partner districts by including study of literary traditions and contemporary works by authors with similar experiences and identities

New Courses Proposed:

TE 306 Legal and Ethical Aspects of Teaching (three credits)

Rationale for Proposal: Legal and ethical aspects of teaching are now a stand-alone competency in the new state certification requirements. As policy and law increasingly hold teachers, rather than districts, personally responsible for classroom environments and the actions and outcomes within them, ensuring that teacher candidates leave the program literate in such issues is essential.

TE 451: Seminar in Teaching and Evaluating Writing (three credits)

Rationale for Proposal: Experts in developing the literacy skills of culturally and linguistically diverse populations argue that texts must be paired with meaningful literacy activities that help students develop literacy skills and place their own writing in conversation with high interest and high prestige texts if literacy instruction is to lead to gains in academic achievement. This new course will facilitate candidate ability to synthesize knowledge gained from their literature and composition coursework into powerful learning experiences.

Dropped Courses:

ENG 300: British Literature 1

Rationale for Drop: Survey of partner districts indicates that very little of the content of the course is included as part of the secondary English curriculum. British literature is not required by the state accrediting body. Elimination of this requirement will make room for literature coursework that better reflects the experiences and identities of the students in partner districts.

Unrestricted English electives (300 level or above) (12 credits)

Rationale for Drop: Subject matter knowledge for ELA teacher preparation should align with partner district curricula, include knowledge of the discipline of English studies and epistemic practices within that discipline, emphasize the application of knowledge to practice, and align with the experiences and identities of P-12 students in partner districts by including study of literary traditions and contemporary works by authors with similar experiences and identities. Allowing unrestricted choice of English electives means that secondary ELA teacher candidates will have idiosyncratic subject matter preparation that may or may not include the above necessary elements.

5

COURSE ALIGNMENT

Introduction

The courses in an academically based teacher preparation program are aligned to the conceptual elements of the teacher preparation program, including philosophical stance, theoretical perspective, and epistemic practices. Alignment is informed by state and national standards for educator preparation, the mission of the institution where the teacher preparation program is located, the needs of partner districts, and specific licensure requirements (Flores, 2016). Alignment occurs within courses, across courses, and between courses and clinical experiences. Proper alignment addresses consistent problems of practice in preservice teacher preparation including idiosyncratic practices, lack of transparency, curricular incoherence, curriculum instability, and developmental discontinuity. The purposeful alignment of course-work ensures that programs are characterized by coherence, continuity, consistency, and trustworthiness.

This chapter is focused on course alignment and misalignment as represented in the research and scholarly literature and in practice in teacher preparation program design. The discussion in this chapter presents a process and a course alignment document, for engaging faculty in course alignment. This process involves methodical alignment of professional knowledge within individual courses and across courses and clinical experiences in the teacher preparation program.

Addressing Persistent Problems of Practice through Course Alignment

The problems of practice addressed in the course alignment process are related to the central characteristics (coherence, continuity, consistency, and trustworthiness) and instrumental characteristics (collaboration, interrelatedness of conceptual and structural elements, and systematic data collection) of academically based teacher preparation. Course alignment is an approach to addressing persistent problems of practice in teaching and teacher preparation related to the use of intuitive and idiosyncratic preferences; identifying, developing, and using valid and reliable teaching practices; purposeful and productive course sequencing; and building the public trust.

Historically, teaching and learning to teach have too often been intuitive and idiosyncratic, rather than based on the best available theory, research, and evidence from practice. This has thwarted efforts to identify valid and reliable teaching practices and approaches for attaining teaching competence during preservice teacher preparation. In an academically based teacher preparation program, valid and reliable practices for teaching and teacher preparation are developed and refined through systematic course alignment; evidence from candidates' work in understanding and applying the knowledge base presented in the program; and data collected from candidates' application of academic knowledge to practice in clinical experiences. The reliability of the data collected in a teacher preparation program depends on the extent to which specific central characteristics exist, including coherence, continuity, consistency, and trustworthiness. Developing valid and reliable practices for teaching and teaching preparation is essential for improving learning outcomes in P-12 schools.

In the previous chapter, context was discussed as the central organizing factor in the basic knowledge base framework for teaching and learning. Including diversity as a cross-cutting theme that is part of each course, ensures that candidates learn the power of context in the application of knowledge related to learners, learning, pedagogy, and subject matter. This will assist candidates in learning to identify and apply valid and reliable teaching practices for different populations of students in various school contexts. Using the teaching cycle and the learning cycle that are part of *teaching as an interpretive practice* and the inquiry stance of observation, documentation, analysis and interpretation for practice ensure that candidates continuously refine their practice such that every child has opportunities for meeting expectations for grade level and subject matter. Providing opportunities for candidates to use valid and reliable teaching practices for P-12 students from diverse cultural and experiential backgrounds addresses the persistent problem of disparities in learning outcomes based on race and social class.

The alignment of course objectives and learning experiences across courses ensures that knowledge for teaching is interconnected, developmental, cumulative, and increasingly complex. This helps to avoid what Rennert-Ariev (2008) described as incoherence:

> [Teacher candidates] were presented with a seemingly scattered array of conceptual alternatives that made it difficult for them to find a central idea that catalyzed their intellectual efforts. Instead, the program didn't really

stand for anything other than, in one faculty's words, "the amalgamation of the people who happen to be teaching in it at any given moment."

(p. 132)

The program conditions Rennert-Ariev (2008) described renders competent teaching elusive for many novice teachers. However, the purpose, theory, and epistemic practices in the conceptual elements of academically based teacher preparation, and that frame the course alignment process described in this chapter, represent the central ideas that provide meaning for the knowledge and experiences in courses and clinical experiences.

Finally, the public trust in elementary and secondary education, the teaching profession, and teacher preparation vacillates based, in part, on the conditions and outcomes of school practices. Building strong public trust in education and the teaching profession is significantly influenced by the strength of the knowledge base for teaching and learning to teach. Course alignment can reveal the strengths and weaknesses in the knowledge base and provide opportunities for adjustments. Questions that will assist teacher educators in examining the strength of the knowledge base include: What evidence will support the validity and reliability of that portion of the knowledge base addressed in each course? What evidence from course assignments reveal the integrity of across course alignment supporting the claim that knowledge is cumulative and increasingly complex? How will faculty determine when the knowledge base needs to be adjusted and what adjustments are needed.

The Process of Course Alignment

The knowledge base for teaching is the basis for professional practice. Professional teaching practice is only as strong as the supporting knowledge base. Weaknesses in the knowledge base contribute to unreliable teaching practices and disappointing P-12 student academic performance. The course alignment process can reveal strengths and weaknesses in the knowledge base and provide opportunities for adjustments.

The knowledge base in teacher preparation is delivered through a variety of formats including courses, modules, independent study, online and in-person group study. While this chapter describes an approach using examples from university-based coursework, the approach can be adapted for teacher preparation programs in different contexts. The content of the knowledge base is not altered by the format. The knowledge base can be organized such that it can be moved from one format to another.

Teacher preparation programs have conceptual and structural elements with supporting factors as described in Chapter 3. In a well-designed teacher preparation program, these elements are interrelated and coordinated. For example, the interrelationship among courses and between courses and clinical experiences is an important aspect of program coherence. Transparency in course development facilitates course alignment and contributes to program coherence. The work of developing program coherence requires collaboration among teacher education faculty, faculty across campus, practitioners, and other stakeholders.

The course alignment process has two parts, *within course alignment* and *across course alignment*. Within course alignment refers to the relationship among state and national standards, course objectives, course assignments, and learning resources. Alignment across courses is focused on the relationship among courses and between courses and clinical experiences, purposeful redundancy for developing professional skills and habits of mind; and ensuring that all state and national standards are adequately addressed. Across course alignment addresses the interrelationship among courses and the developmental sequencing.

Alignment across courses requires that faculty members know the course content and learning experiences for all the required courses in the teacher preparation program (Bain & Moje, 2012; Darling-Hammond, 2006). It is important for faculty to understand the purpose and context for clinical experiences, and for clinical supervisors and mentor teachers to know the habits of mind, knowledge, and skills candidates bring to the field from university coursework (Grossman, Hammerness, McDonald, & Ronfeldt, 2008; Korthagen, Loughran, & Russell, 2006; Warner, 2016). The development of complex professional knowledge and skills requires a purposefully planned, transparent approach.

The course alignment process begins with an agreed upon format for within course alignment. The Course Alignment Document is used to guide aligning and redesigning existing courses and as an initial template for the design of new courses (see Appendix A). This format includes five components:

1.   course information,
2.   state and national standards,
3.   course objectives,
4.   course assignments, and
5.   resources.

Course information includes the course title and number, a list of licensure programs that require the course, and a course description. It is important for the course description to appropriately represent the course content and focus, including language related to the course objectives. The state or national standards and competencies identified for the course are directly related to the course description. In the sample provided, the course is aligned to the InTASC standards (CCSO, 2016). The state and national standards selected are translated into course objectives or learning outcomes appropriate for the subject matter of the course. Course assignments that will provide candidates with the learning experiences necessary to master the objectives are developed. These course assignments enable candidates to develop the knowledge and skills represented in the course objectives, conduct observations, or to apply knowledge to practice. The resources provide opportunities for focused inquiry into the research and scholarly literature, viewing video examples, examining primary source documents, and making observations. To stabilize the knowledge base, faculty are encouraged to develop an agreement that resources are the only elements that can be changed by an individual instructor without the consent of the teacher preparation faculty as a unit. Resources may be changed so long as they continue to support the agreed upon course objectives and assignments.

Consistent with the program explication process described in the previous chapter, the alignment process takes into consideration university policies, procedures, and deadlines for catalog changes. The alignment process usually results in revised course descriptions and, possibly, the drafting of new courses; deadlines relating to state and national accreditation; faculty workload, particularly if individual faculty are serving as leads for multiple courses; and time for external collaboration. The number of courses and faculty in a program can be staggered to increase manageability. Additionally, faculty will need to identify appropriate resources for each course.

Within Course Alignment

The process of within course alignment involves establishing the relationship between state and national standards, course objectives, course assignments, and learning resources. It is used to facilitate both the development of new courses and the redesign of existing courses.

Faculty Leadership for Course Alignment

This approach requires that a course alignment document is completed for each course in the teacher preparation program. Lead faculty members are selected based on expertise and experience with the portion of the professional knowledge base for which each course is responsible. For example, the lead faculty member for the sample course described in Appendix A had experience providing districts with professional development on data teaming and a research agenda focused on classroom assessment. If the teacher preparation program lacks a faculty member with a depth of knowledge relating to a particular standard or competency, then a faculty member interested in learning more may be assigned with the expectation for collaboration with other experts in the field. Alternately, a program may contract with an external expert to develop a particular course and have the course vetted by other experts. When taking inventory of faculty expertise, program redesign leaders consider the possibility that P-12 district partners and faculty from other units on campus may have the requisite knowledge.

Collaboration and Information Gathering

The course alignment process requires faculty to gather specific information from curriculum documents, university catalogue, university website, and from other members of the program faculty. Lead faculty need licensure or degree requirements and Program Explication Documents (described in the previous chapter) for all licensure areas offered by the unit. This will identify courses shared across two or more licensure areas.

Most courses have been designed for a specific licensure area such as elementary education, and later included in other licensure areas such as middle or secondary education. This practice is acceptable when the course is adjusted to ensure appropriate relevance for each licensure area, but such adjustments do not always occur. This is especially true when the faculty member responsible for developing or teaching the course lacks expertise in one or more of the licensure areas served by the course. During the course alignment process, lead faculty members consider all licensure areas served by each course and collaborate with other faculty members with expertise related to a particular licensure area or level. In the example course provided in Appendix A, the lead faculty member had expertise and experience in assessment and data at the middle and secondary levels, but consulted with an elementary faculty member on the ways assessment practices might differ at the elementary level.

Lead faculty members meet with faculty across the teacher preparation program to establish consensus about program needs and expectations for a particular course. Frequently, individuals feel ownership of one or more courses rather than viewing the courses as integral components of the teacher education curriculum that is the responsibility of the teacher education faculty as a unit. Consensus by the faculty as a unit regarding the expectations for each course is necessary at the beginning of the course alignment process. Possible questions the lead faculty member can ask of faculty from the different licensure areas using a shared course include:

- What habits of mind are candidates expected to develop during their experiences in this course?
- What are candidates expected to know and be able to do after completing this course?
- What learning experiences are most important for candidates to gain from this course?
- What knowledge and skills essential for a beginning teacher in this specific licensure area should be included in this course?

Based on responses from these questions, lead faculty synthesize the expectations for specific courses.

In addition, lead faculty members undertake a survey of scholarly literature on the course subject matter to determine the best available research, theory, and evidence from practice that supports the propositional, conditional, and procedural knowledge for teaching and teacher preparation. The lead faculty member already possesses significant expertise in the subject matter of the course. However, new knowledge based on research evidence, innovations, and updates to advances in understanding existing knowledge are important for even experts in the field when designing and updating courses. This survey of literature is even more important if the lead faculty member has limited expertise in the subject matter for the course. Further, lead faculty need copies of national accreditation standards, content standards from professional organizations related to each course, and state licensure regulations.

Aligning to Epistemic Practices

In academically based teacher preparation, epistemic practices derived from the theoretical perspective for the program are evident at all levels of the program. As discussed in earlier chapters, epistemic practices are purposefully developed sequences of interrelated and repetitive actions that establish routines; create order and predictability; and develop habits of mind and behaviors that increase accuracy and efficiency in an approach, completing a task, and achieving a goal or objective. Assignments and learning experiences in courses and clinical experiences are structured to require candidates to engage in epistemic practices in the process of meeting learning outcomes. As faculty develop or review assignments during the within course alignment process, they ensure compatibility with and inclusion of program epistemic practices.

Aligning the Knowledge Base to Standards

Based on the information gathered from documents and discussions, lead faculty revise existing or draft new course descriptions synthesizing program expectations, the scholarly literature, and evidence from practice. Comparison of the course description to state and national standards helps identify specific standards related to the course subject matter. The matrix of standards, mandates, and program requirements described in the previous chapter can help facilitate this process.

Modules

Learning outcomes, assignments, and resources can be linked to form learning modules. Each learning outcome has a core set of resources that comprise the professional knowledge base related to that outcome. Each learning outcome also has at least one assignment or primary learning experience designed to facilitate candidates' ability to apply knowledge to practice. These three components together form a learning module. Two illustrative modules are represented in the sample in Appendix A. Usually, courses will contain three to five learning modules. Organizing the content of teacher preparation into modules supports alignment across courses and provides flexibility that facilitates adjustments and corrections in the knowledge base. Addressing a standard or regulation can require reframing a module within a course, adding, or replacing a module, or moving a module from one course to another.

Drafting Course Learning Outcomes

The statements of specific objectives or learning outcomes for a course are informed by state and national standards, the synthesis of the scholarly literature related to the subject matter of the course, evidence from practice, and the conceptual elements for the teacher preparation program. When drafting or revising course learning outcomes, lead faculty begin by reviewing the conceptual elements of the preservice teacher preparation program. These elements are based on a programmatic understanding of competent teaching and a vision of the kind of educators program graduates will become, how graduates will contribute to the local community, and the impact graduates will have on the P-12 students. Based on this understanding, lead faculty consider what program graduates need to know and be able to do related to the specific course content to be prepared for teaching in P-12 classrooms.

Program epistemic practices are reflected in the learning outcomes of courses throughout the program. For example, the faculty that developed the example in Appendix A agreed on a philosophical stance related to developing teacher competency to meet the needs of diverse students in urban schools. The program embraced the theoretical perspective of *learning teaching as an interpretive process*, which included the epistemic practices of focused inquiry, directed observation, and guided practice (discussed in depth in Chapter 3). Given this programmatic focus, the course learning outcomes for TE 300 center on candidates engaging in focused inquiry and directed observation to gather and analyze data in diverse urban classrooms, and guided practice in developing assessments to administer during clinical experiences. The premise that teaching is highly contextual and that the role of assessment is to help teachers understand and plan for meeting the needs of specific learners in specific contexts undergirds this example. A different teacher preparation program with a different view of competent teaching—perhaps a view that considers good teaching to be faithful and consistent replication of a particular set of research-based teaching moves—would likely develop very different learning outcomes in its version of an assessment course. Program conceptual elements carry over from learning outcomes into the assignments developed to facilitate candidates meeting specific outcomes.

Designing Assignments and Learning Experiences

Shulman (2005) argued that the signature pedagogies of a profession are based on a shared conceptualization of the best way to learn a body of professional knowledge that include the dispositions, values, and habits of mind necessary for that profession. Common learning experiences in preservice teacher preparation include systematic observation; case analysis (both written and video); case study writing; planning of learning experiences; interpretation, reflection, or analysis of enacted learning experiences; and microteaching (Darling-Hammond & Bransford, 2005; Darling-Hammond & Hammerness, 2002; McDonald, Kazemi, & Kavanaugh, 2013).

Well-designed assignments are essential for program coherence, consistency, and continuity. Assignments in academically based preservice teacher preparation are consistent with the philosophical stance and the theoretical perspective of the program, incorporate epistemic practices, and connect to clinical experiences. For example, a teacher preparation program grounded in the theoretical perspective of *learning teaching as an interpretive process* include the epistemic practices of focused inquiry, directed observation, and guided practice, and course assignments facilitate engagement in these practices.

The first sample assignment on the example included in Appendix A requires candidates to engage in directed observation and documentation related to the school context, students' life experiences, and students' academic backgrounds to construct an electronic portfolio of essential information to use in planning instruction for a specific group of learners in a specific context. Prior to candidates beginning this assignment, course instructors employ course resources to facilitate focused inquiry into the rationale and approach for data collection, and the interpretation and translation of the data for application to practice. Later experiences and assignments in the course provide opportunities for application to practice in a clinical context the findings from data collection. These core assignments and experiences form the epistemic practices that are common across all modules in the course. Once the course has been approved by the teacher preparation faculty as a unit, the assignments and experiences are not changed or discarded without deliberation and approval by the faculty unit.

Learning Resources

The resources compiled in the course alignment process form the literal professional knowledge base for an academically based teacher preparation program. Candidates need propositional, conditional, and procedural knowledge for application to practice in all courses. This requires academic knowledge that includes research demonstrating the conditions under which knowledge is applicable, learning the procedures for application and making observation of application on video or in classrooms. Selection of learning resources is directly connected to candidate learning outcomes.

The resources listed in the second module on the sample alignment document in Appendix A are illustrative of the various types of knowledge and the connection to assignments and learning objectives. Penuel and Shepard's (2016) research synthesis on assessment and teaching provides candidates with propositional and conditional knowledge regarding theories, principles, and types of assessment and the connection to teaching and learning. Tomlinson and McTighe's (2006) volume on differentiation and instructional planning provides candidates with procedural knowledge necessary to develop assessments for learning goals. Together, these resources represent a body of knowledge, the application of which will allow candidates to complete the assignment and meet the learning outcome listed in Module 2 of the sample.

Of the three module components—learning outcome, assignment, and resources—the resources are the most flexible. While course learning outcomes and assignments are not changed without deliberation and consensus across the teacher preparation program, learning resources may be adjusted so long as they continue to support the agreed upon assignments and objectives.

Across Course Alignment

The second component of the alignment process is across course alignment. Alignment across courses refers to the interrelationship among courses and the developmental sequencing of courses into a coherent teacher preparation program. The process of across course alignment occurs following completion of within course alignment for all courses in an academically based preservice teacher preparation program. When course alignment documents have been completed for all courses, they are made available to faculty across the program for deliberation and across course alignment.

Developmental Sequencing

As indicated throughout this volume, the courses and clinical experiences in academically based teacher preparation are developmentally sequenced and interconnected to support cumulative and increasingly complex understanding of the relationship among learning, learner characteristics, subject matter, pedagogy, and learning outcomes. The process of program explication discussed in the previous chapter included the drafting of a preliminary developmental sequence for courses. During the alignment process, that developmental sequence is refined.

This aspect of the teacher preparation program design is conceptualized as a sequence of developmental blocks composed of related courses and associated clinical experiences (See Figure 5.1 for a sample block from a secondary English licensure program). Each block builds on the next to constitute a coherent program of academically based teacher preparation. The role and structure of clinical experiences are discussed in detail in Chapter 6.

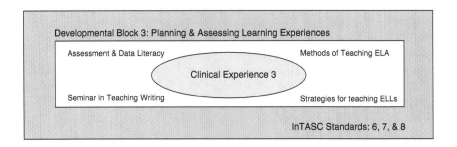

The courses in a developmental block have complementary and interconnected assignments and experiences; and are linked to the same state and national standards that have been appropriately interpreted for the subject matter of each course.

FIGURE 5.1 Sample developmental block

The framework of professional knowledge described in the previous chapter (see Figure 4.1) serves as an initial guide for assigning courses to specific blocks. The big ideas in that framework are learners, learning, subject matter, pedagogy, and context. A well-designed program includes purposeful redundancy and graduated levels of complexity for developing professional skills and habits of mind. In the final block, which includes advanced clinical practice (discussed in more detail in the Chapter 6), candidates are expected to develop and demonstrate competence in all areas of classroom teaching. During the advanced clinical experience, candidates synthesize professional knowledge from all parts of the framework and demonstrate the skills necessary to apply that knowledge to practice in a particular context. Program designers collaborate on backwards mapping to order courses in a sequence leading to candidates meeting that goal.

Using course alignment documents, learning outcomes from courses linked to the same big idea are compared, and courses are sequenced depending on the cumulative and progressive complexity of skill and knowledge necessary to meet the outcomes. Succeeding blocks require more refined synthesis and elaborated application of knowledge and skill. Determinations are made about where in the sequence different elements of the big ideas are introduced, reinforced, and elaborated.

Epistemic Practices

During the across course alignment process, faculty consider the integration of epistemic practices across the program. In an academically based teacher preparation program, epistemic practices derived from the theoretical perspective on learning to teach are evident at all levels of the program. During across course alignment, faculty review the assignments from each block of the program to ensure that agreed upon epistemic practices are included and reinforced from the beginning of the program to the end. As candidates move through the program, the engagement with epistemic practices increases in complexity. If epistemic practices are not evident in parts of the program, faculty collaborate to adjust assignments and experiences in each block to emphasize those practices.

Accreditation Standards and Cross-Cutting Themes

While engaging in the across course alignment process, program designers ensure that all required state and national standards are adequately addressed. Course alignment documents indicate which courses have incorporated specific state or national standards. Examining all courses in a program linked to a particular standard allows the faculty to determine whether each standard is adequately addressed.

During the across course alignment process, program designers consider cross-cutting themes that may be necessary components of the program philosophical stance or may be required by state or national accreditors. Cross-cutting themes are incorporated into every block of the program and in most courses. Examples of cross-cutting themes include *diversity* and *technology*, both of which are required for programs seeking national accreditation from CAEP. Diversity is an important cross-cutting theme for the secondary English licensure program that is used as an example in this and the previous chapter. Diversity is important because it is required by CAEP and, more importantly, because meeting the needs of diverse learners is central to the program philosophical stance. As such, knowledge of diversity is integrated into professional education coursework, subject matter coursework, and clinical experiences throughout the program.

During the across course alignment process, program designers look for evidence of cross-cutting themes in learning outcomes, assignments, and resources in all blocks of the program. If evidence for cross-cutting themes is lacking, faculty collaborate to suggest additional resources, adjustments to assignments or outcomes, and, in some cases, the development of new modules.

Faculty review and deliberation throughout the across course alignment process can reveal gaps and unintentional redundancies in the program. Addressing gaps may require revision of courses or modules or the development of new courses or modules. Redundancies are carefully considered to determine if they are intentional and purposeful. Purposeful redundancies include elaboration on previously established knowledge and opportunities to apply the knowledge in new contexts. Unintended redundancies are addressed by the replacement or removal of assignments or modules, or the elimination of a course. These decisions are made collaboratively and with transparency, and with all program stakeholders involved in the process.

Alignment within Blocks

Once courses have been organized into blocks, all assignments in each block are considered together to reveal ways in which assignments across courses are complementary and interconnected. Faculty discuss whether conceptual or structural adjustments to assignments will provide more coherent learning experiences for candidates in that block. As discussed earlier in this chapter, each course in an academically based teacher preparation program has at least one assignment linked to clinical experience. These assignments require careful scrutiny because of the influence on the arrangement and content of the clinical experience required for that block.

As an example, the developmental block illustrated in Figure 5.1 is composed of a mid-level clinical experience and four courses:

1. Assessment and Data Literacy,
2. Methods of Teaching English Language Arts,
3. Seminar in Teaching and Evaluating Writing, and
4. Strategies for Teaching English Language Learners (ELLs).

An assignment in the methods Course 2 is to develop an ELA lesson for the learners in the classroom in which a candidate is placed for the mid-level clinical experience. For the course on teaching ELLs (Course 4), candidates write a commentary detailing the ways the instructional strategies they employed in the lesson for the methods course met the needs of the ELLs in the clinical experience classroom. In the assessment course (Course 1), candidates develop an assessment plan to complement the lesson designed in Course 2. Finally, for the writing seminar (Course 3), candidates collect writing samples generated during the lesson for Course 2 and collaborate with peers in evaluating the writing samples. Connecting assignments in such a complementary manner during the across course alignment process contributes to a powerful and coherent teacher preparation experience.

Once faculty have agreed on the positioning of a course within a developmental sequence, the course position is not changed without faculty deliberation and consensus. Repositioning a course in a developmental sequence is a complex endeavor that can require revisiting and redesigning learning outcomes, assignments, and connections to clinical experience for the course being repositioned. Repositioning a course can involve changes in other courses in both the block from which the course is removed and the block to which the course is being repositioned.

Conclusion

This chapter described an alignment process to facilitate coherence, continuity, consistency, and trustworthiness in an academically based teacher preparation program. Course alignment makes possible a complementary and interconnected sequence of learning experiences that advance candidates' progress towards competent teaching. Course alignment is an approach to addressing persistent problems of practice in teaching and teacher preparation related to the use of intuitive and idiosyncratic preferences; identifying, developing, and using valid and reliable teaching practices; purposeful and productive course sequencing; and building the public trust. The process includes both within course alignment and across course alignment. The Course Alignment Document facilitates collaborative faculty decision making in course and program design.

References

Bain, R. B. & Moje, E. B. (2012). Mapping the teacher education terrain for novices. *Phi Delta Kappan*, 93, 62–65.

Council of Chief State School Officers (CCSO) (2016). *Interstate teacher assessment and support consortium* (InTASC). http://programs.ccsso.org/projects/interstate_new_teacher_assessment_and_support_consortium/.

Darling-Hammond, L. (2006). *Powerful teacher education: Lessons from exemplary programs*. San Francisco, CA: Jossey-Bass.

Darling-Hammond, L. & Bransford, J. (2005). *Preparing teachers for a changing world: what teachers should learn and be able to do*. San Francisco, CA: Jossey-Bass.

Darling-Hammond, L. & Hammerness, K. (2002). Toward a pedagogy of cases in teacher education. *Teaching Education*, 13 (2), 37–41.

Flores, M. A. (2016). Teacher education curriculum. In J. Loughran & M. L. Hamilton (Eds.), *International handbook of teacher education*, vol. 1 (pp. 187–230). Singapore: Springer.

Grossman, P., Hammerness, K., Mcdonald, M., & Ronfeldt, M. (2008). Constructing coherence: Structural predictors of perceptions of coherence in NYC teacher education programs. *Journal of Teacher Education*, 59 (4), 273–287.

Korthagen, F., Loughran, J., & Russell, T. (2006). Developing fundamental principles for teacher education programs and practices. *Teaching and Teacher Education*, 22 (1), 1020–1041.

McDonald, M., Kazemi, E., & Kavanagh, S. S. (2013). Core practices and pedagogies of teacher education: A call for a common language and collective activity. *Journal of Teacher Education*, 64 (5), 378–386.

Penuel, W. R. & Shepard, L. A. (2016). Assessment and teaching. In D. H. Gitomer & C. A. Bell (Eds.), *Handbook of research on teaching* (5th ed., pp. 787–850). Washington, DC: American Educational Research Association.

Rennert-Ariev, P. (2008). The hidden curriculum of performance-based teacher education. *Teachers College Record*, 110 (1), 105–138.

Shulman, L. S. (2005). Signature pedagogies in the professions. *Daedalus*, 134 (3), 52–59.

Tomlinson, C. A. & McTighe, J. (2006). *Integrating differentiated instruction & understanding by design: Connecting content and kids*. ASCD.

Warner, C. K. (2016). Constructions of excellent teaching: Identity tensions in preservice English teachers. *National Teacher Education Journal*, 9 (1), 5–16.

Appendix A: Sample Course Alignment Document

Course Information

Course Title

TE 300 Assessment and Data Literacy

Licensure Programs

Elementary, Middle School (all), Secondary Education (all), K-12 (all)

Course Description

Data collection and assessment strategies—including formative, summative, formal, and informal—to be used in developing student learning profiles, planning learning experiences, and monitoring student progress toward academic goals. Topics include the impact of assessment on equitable education for diverse learners, critical observation and questioning, basic qualitative and quantitative data analysis, working with data teams, collaboration/communication with families and other educational stakeholders, setting and monitoring learning goals, and the ethics of data collection and sharing.

Standards and Competencies

InTASC Standards

Standard #6: Assessment. The teacher understands and uses multiple methods of assessment to engage learners in their own growth, to monitor learner progress, and to guide the teacher's and learner's decision making.
Standard #10: Leadership and Collaboration. The teacher seeks appropriate leadership roles and opportunities to take responsibility for student learning, to collaborate with learners, families, colleagues, other school professionals, and community members to ensure learner growth, and to advance the profession.

Modules

Module 1

Learning outcome 1: Teacher candidates will collect and analyze academic, social, and cultural data about a class of diverse learners in order to develop a class profile for use in planning instruction.

Assignment 1: Develop an electronic portfolio of essential data about the context and students in your clinical experience. Your profile should have at least three sections—contextual information, student experiential information, and student academic information[1]—and should contain individual entries for each student in your class.

Resources for Module 1

Hollins, E. R. (2015). Learning about diverse populations of students. In *Culture in School Learning: Revealing the Deep Meaning* (3rd ed., pp. 65–90). New York: Routledge.

Moll, L., Amanti, C., Neff, D., and Gonzalez, N. (1992). Funds of knowledge for teaching: Using a qualitative approach to connect homes and classrooms. *Theory into Practice, 31*(2), 132–141.

Module 2

Learning outcome 2: Teacher candidates will develop an assessment plan to determine student learning needs in relation to a particular content standard in a specific urban classroom, paying particular attention to social, emotional, and cognitive development.

Assignment 2: Work with your cooperating teacher to develop a learning objective based on specific standards that you will be responsible for teaching at some point during the semester. Then develop a pre-assessment that will generate the data necessary for you to determine each of your students' individual readiness to meet that learning objective, and a post-assessment that will help you determine whether or not each of your students has met that learning objective after engaging in a learning experience targeting that objective. You will also suggest at least 3 formative assessment strategies that might be used throughout the course of a learning experience in order to monitor individual student progress toward the objective. While designing these assessments, be sure to consider whether any modifications or accommodations might be necessary to ensure accessibility and validity for all your students. Lastly, you will administer your pre-assessment and then develop a graphic representation of the trends in the data you gathered (this will be used to plan a learning experience later in the course). In a three-page commentary, describe why the assessment choices you made are appropriate for your students, your context, and your learning objective.

Resources for Module 2

Penuel, W. R. and Shepard, L. A. (2016). Assessment and teaching. In D. H. Gitomer & C. A. Bell (Eds.), *Handbook of research on teaching* (5th ed., pp. 787–850). Washington, DC: American Educational Research Association.

Tomlinson, C. A. and McTighe, J. (2006). *Integrating differentiated instruction & understanding by design: Connecting content and kids.* ASCD.

Note

1 Based on the Reflective Interpretive Inquiry (RIQ) detailed in Chapter 4 of Hollins (2015)

6

CLINICAL EXPERIENCES IN AUTHENTIC CONTEXTS

Introduction

This chapter is focused on clinical experiences as the bridge between academic knowledge and competent teaching. This discussion brings to the forefront the ubiquitous, yet often obscured, essential practices and habits of mind that support competent teaching and the essential tools and processes. The approach presented addresses both the process for learning to teach and for guidance by teacher educators and mentor teachers. The examples of practices and tools are presented to illustrate a material factor or an approach that can be replicated or modified as appropriate for different teacher preparation programs.

The approaches and tools presented in this chapter are consistent with recommendations included in the report of the Blue Ribbon Panel formed by the National Council for the Accreditation of Teacher Education (NCATE) (2010), the report of the Clinical Practice Commission of the American Association of Colleges of Teacher Education (AACTE) (2018), the National Board for Professional Teaching Standards' Five Core Propositions, and *Lessons from the Teachers for a New Era Project* (McDiarmid & Caprino, 2018). Each of these reports described clinical experiences as pivotal in teacher preparation.

Developing teaching competence is part of a national concern for the quality of education available in the society that enables individuals to care and provide for themselves and their families, citizens to contribute and participate in a democratic society, and that supports the academic and intellectual resources needed by the nation. The present conditions in the nation's public schools as described in the introduction to this book require redesigning teacher preparation programs. In describing the task of redesigning teacher preparation, the National Council for the Accreditation of Teacher Education (NCATE) Blue Ribbon Panel stated that:

The education of teachers in the United States needs to be turned upside down. To prepare effective teachers for 21st century classrooms, teacher education must shift away from a norm which emphasizes academic preparation and course work loosely linked to school-based experiences. Rather, it must move to programs that are fully grounded in clinical practice and interwoven with academic content and professional courses.

(2010, p. ii)

The NCATE Blue Ribbon Panel identified ten design principles for clinically based preparation to guide the redesign of preservice teacher preparation programs that include:

1. student learning is the focus
2. clinical preparation is integrated throughout every facet of teacher education in a dynamic way
3. a candidate's progress and the elements of a preparation program are continuously judged on the basis of data
4. programs prepare teachers who are expert in content and how to teach it and are also innovators, collaborators and problem solvers
5. candidates learn in an interactive professional community
6. clinical educators and coaches are rigorously selected and prepared and drawn from both higher education and the P-12 sector
7. specific sites are designated and funded to support embedded clinical preparation
8. technology applications foster high-impact preparation
9. a powerful R & D agenda and systematic gathering and use of data supports continuous improvement in teacher preparation
10. strategic partnerships are imperative for powerful clinical preparation.

These design principles describe the *conditions necessary* for candidates to engage in the process of learning to teach and for developing teaching competence.

The AACTE Clinical Practice Commission (2018) affirmed the NCATE Blue Ribbon Panel design principles for clinically based teacher preparation and added a guiding conceptual model with six steps and ten proclamations. Central in the Clinical Practice Commission report are university-school partnerships and learning in P-12 schools. This is evident in the statement that:

Good clinical practice design begins with the learning needs of the PK-12 students. Identifying the specific needs of the instructional context requires working from the inside out and transforming the way both school-based and university-based educators plan curriculum and instruction.

(p. 26)

The AACTE guiding conceptual model describes the interrelationship among courses and clinical experiences in a developmental sequence. This type of structure is incorporated into the organization of early and mid-level clinical experiences in this chapter. The ten proclamations are integrated across the teacher preparation program described in this book.

The National Board for Professional Teaching Standards was established in 1987 for the purpose of defining and recognizing accomplished teaching. A rigorous peer assessment process is used for national certification for accomplished teaching. The standards for national board certification are based on five core propositions that describe the essential attributes for competent and accomplished teaching that include:

1.   teachers are committed to students and their learning,
2.   teachers know the subjects they teach and how to teach those subjects to students,
3.   teachers are responsible for managing and monitoring student learning,
4.   teachers think systematically about their practice and learn from experience, and
5.   teachers are members of learning communities.

The approach to clinical experiences described in this chapter requires that candidates demonstrate the attributes incorporated in these core propositions.

The Teachers for a New Era Project (TNE) was a national initiative sponsored by the Carnegie Corporation of New York that began in 2001 for the purpose of improving teacher preparation. The TNE addressed three persistent problems of practice in teacher preparation that included:

•   providing evidence for the effect of university-based teacher preparation on candidates' and teachers' classroom performance,
•   raising the status of teacher preparation on university campuses and improving collaboration among teacher education faculty and arts and sciences faculty, and
•   engaging K-12 school practitioners as equal partners in supporting candidates and novice teachers in achieving full teaching competency.

The implementation of TNE employed a residency model for teacher preparation programs based on three design principles that included:

1.   "a teacher education program should be guided by a respect for evidence,"
2.   "faculty in the disciplines of the arts and sciences should be fully engaged in the education of prospective teachers, especially in the areas of subject matter understanding and general and liberal education," and
3.   "education should be understood as an academically taught clinical practice profession."

(TNE, 2001, p. 4)

The initial project was a longitudinal study involving 11 university-based teacher preparation programs. The design principles guided the work in the 11 participating institutions.

The authors McDiarmid and Caprino (2018) reported on four of the 11 institutions that participated in TNE. This was a longitudinal study that sought to address specific issues related to changes in teacher preparation programs resulting from the project, factors that influenced implementation of the design principles, and knowledge gained from institutions participating in the project. Each participating institution demonstrated that change is possible, that existing challenges can be resolved, and that it is possible to collaborate with public schools to improve student learning outcomes. The participating institutions used different approaches in addressing the three design principles and the data and strategies were not fully explained in the report. Each of the programs in the report retained the apprenticeship model in the teacher residency and only one reported a curriculum review to determine what candidates were learning in courses.

These three reports provide postulates for developing a more detailed conceptualization of clinical experiences. This chapter presents a conceptualization of clinical experiences grounded in a constructivist theoretical perspective referred to as *teaching as an interpretive practice/process* delineated in four parts, purpose and theory, context, organization, and monitoring progress.

Purpose and Theory in Authentic Clinical Experiences

Chapter 3 focused on the conceptual and structural elements in teacher preparation program design. The conceptual elements included the philosophical stance, theoretical perspective on learning to teach, professional knowledge and skills, and epistemic practices. The structural elements included admission practices, alignment of academic and clinical experiences, school partnerships, assessment of professional knowledge and skills, and program evaluation. This chapter extends the discussion of the relationship between conceptual and structural elements in teacher preparation program design. Clinical experiences comprise one of the structural elements that applies the conceptual elements.

Clinical experiences provide candidates with the context for *application to practice* of each conceptual element included in the teacher preparation program. In a well-designed teacher preparation program, each conceptual element is included in coursework and each course has a clinical experience assignment. The academic knowledge and clinical experiences are developmentally sequenced and interconnected to support cumulative and increasingly complex understanding of the relationship among learning, learner characteristics, subject matter, pedagogy, and learning outcomes.

Philosophical Stance

The general purpose for clinical experiences is for candidates to engage in the *application to practice* of academic knowledge in facilitating the academic, psychological, and social development of children and youth in P-12 schools. The philosophical stance guides the selection of the context for clinical experiences. The philosophical stance addresses who is being prepared to teach what knowledge and skills to whom, for what purpose, and the expected impact on individuals, their communities, and the larger society. An authentic context situates clinical experiences within the *milieu of the target population* for which candidates are being prepared to teach. This promotes developing deep knowledge of the relationship among learning, learner characteristics, subject matter, pedagogy, and learning outcomes. In this application to practice, candidates learn the *process for contextualizing* learning experiences and teaching practices for a specific population of learners. The practice of contextualizing learning is applicable to other contexts and populations. In this approach, candidates learn to address all aspects of diversity among students.

Theoretical Perspective

The theoretical perspective in *teaching as an interpretive practice/process* (TIP) and learning teaching as an interpretive practice/process (L-TIP) significantly differ from the traditional *cognitivist* perspective that is highly recognizable in clinical experiences for teacher preparation. The traditional cognitivist perspective employs a *cognitive apprenticeship* approach to clinical experiences that emphasizes learning to teach through observation, modeling, and approximation in replicating the practices of an experienced teacher. Guidance for clinical experiences in a cognitive apprenticeship include coaching, scaffolding, articulation, and reflection. In contrast, guidance in L-TIP emphasizes the analysis of teaching through interconnecting knowledge of learners, learning, pedagogy, and subject matter. In the cognitive apprentice model, the emphasis appears to be more on a) *teaching as performance* rather than b) *teaching as an interpretive practice* that involves continuously adjusting instruction to better facilitate students' learning experiences and learning outcomes.

Learning to teach as an interpretive practice (L-TIP) employs a constructivist approach to guided practice for developing competent teaching within a context of reciprocal learning for mentors and mentees. Candidates learn to observe, analyze, and adjust teaching practices based on students' responses. Early and mid-level clinical experiences are systematically guided by assessments and embedded course assignments. Advanced clinical practice emphasizes the *application to practice* of the full range of professional knowledge and skills presented in courses across the teacher preparation program. Mentor teachers learn the theory and practices that are foundational for the teacher preparation program, support implementation, and adjust their own teaching practices to better support student learning.

L-TIP engages candidates in the *continuous analysis of teaching and learning* through focused inquiry in their academic work, directed observations in authentic settings related to the focused inquiry, and guided practice in the application to practice of knowledge from focused inquiry and directed observations. Courses and clinical experiences are organized into a purposefully sequenced progression of blocks where academic knowledge and skills are interrelated, cumulative, and increasingly complex (see Chapter 5). Each block has specific learning outcomes and assessments for monitoring and measuring progress in learning to teach.

The learning outcomes in a block are appropriately interpreted for the subject matter of each course positioned in the block. Each course has a clinical experience component related to the professional knowledge and skills in the specific course. The clinical experience engages candidates in directed observation, documentation, analysis, interpretation, and the application of academic knowledge to practice when appropriate. For example, in a course on ethical and legal issues in teaching, candidates are required to review a local school district handbook to examine students' privacy rights. This is an example of the application of academic knowledge to practice.

The approach to clinical experiences is based on a theoretical perspective on learning to teach. This theoretical perspective is modeled for candidates in class meetings, course assignments, and through guidance during clinical experiences. The consistent use of a specific theoretical perspective across courses and clinical experiences supports the development of a cognitive schema that fosters the habits of mind for engaging valid and reliable teaching practices.

Learning teaching as an interpretive process (L-TIP) is mediated by academic knowledge from coursework and specifically designed professional tools and practices. There are six categories of tools associated with this conceptualization of teaching and learning teaching that include:

- knowledge of learners,
- planning,
- instruction,
- curriculum and pedagogy,
- guided practice, and
- assessment.

Examples of tools associated with TIP include a teaching cycle, a learning cycle, student development inventory, student observation inventory, and a class profile. The continuous improvement of teaching practices and student learning outcomes is based on the analysis of teaching and learning using the associated tools. The description and application of these tools are discussed later in this chapter.

Epistemic Practices

Epistemic practices are those purposefully designed reoccurring experiences that develop specific habits of mind, behaviors, and professional practices that are essential for competent teaching. In learning to teach, epistemic practices include focused inquiry, directed observation, and guided practice. Teaching, like other professions, requires consistency in thought and practice to achieve the expected outcomes. In the absence of consistency in professional practices, outcomes are less predictable and solutions to problems of practice are more elusive. Epistemic practices are procedures embedded within the theoretical perspective in a teacher preparation program to facilitate development of the specific cognitive schema and habits of mind that support consistency in applying the best available research, theory, and evidence from practice.

Focused Inquiry

The approach to developing academic knowledge and skills for competent teaching is referred to as focused inquiry. This includes the knowledge of learners, learning, subject matter, and pedagogy that form the basis for the *application of academic knowledge to practice* in teaching and teacher preparation. The *application of academic knowledge to practice* is distributed across courses and clinical experiences, monitored, and assessed over time.

Directed Observation

During initial clinical experiences, candidates focus attention on specific aspects of students' responses to learning experiences and the social context in the classroom through the lens of academic knowledge and skills included in coursework. This is referred to as directed observation. The observation, documentation, and analysis of students' responses to learning experiences support the development of deep knowledge of the relationship among learning, learner characteristics, subject matter, pedagogy and learning outcomes. Mid-level and advanced clinical experiences engage candidates in the application to practice of knowledge and skills for guiding student growth and development.

Guided Practice

Guidance for learning teaching practices is provided incrementally across the teacher preparation program through embedding focused inquiry, directed observation and peripheral participation in P-12 classrooms. These early experiences support candidates in making a transition from the view of teaching from a student perspective to that of a teacher, and in becoming familiar with specific classroom practices and routines. Candidates engage in careful observation and documentation of students' responses to learning experiences and the social context in the classroom through the lens of academic knowledge from coursework. Advanced clinical practice provides opportunities for candidates to develop and demonstrate all aspects of competent teaching. Advanced clinical practice is supported by pre- and post-observation question protocols and an observation checklist.

Context for Clinical Experiences

Maintaining program coherence requires that clinical experiences are consistent with the philosophical stance of the teacher preparation program. This means that community agencies and schools providing opportunities for clinical experiences serve the population for which candidates are being prepared to teach. Schools are not expected to have fully implemented the theoretical perspective incorporated into the teacher preparation program, but they are expected to be amenable to it. Community agencies and schools providing clinical experiences are not expected to be perfect, but they are expected to be committed to continuous improvement and reciprocal benefit from a partnership with the local teacher preparation program provider.

The expectations for a community-school-teacher preparation collaboration requires a clearly delineated agreement among participants based on reciprocal support for the goals and needs of each. The primary goal of the partnership is to impact the quality of life in the local community by improving the quality of education available for children and youth. The partnership is based on shared understanding of the needs of the local community, the role and approach used by each partner, and the relationship among the separate and collective efforts that generate the reciprocal benefit and support.

Teacher educators enter the partnership with knowledge of each member including the challenges and issues faced by the local schools and school districts; the resources, social and political issues in the local community; and the services provided by local agencies to address specific challenges and issues. Teacher educators are prepared to explain to partners how the philosophical stance and specific aspects of the academic knowledge in the teacher preparation program address identifiable needs in the local schools and community. Further, teacher educators are prepared to explain the reciprocal benefit shared among participants that relate to the teacher preparation program. Faculty explain what candidates need to learn and the opportunities for learning required during clinical experiences, and any services that will be provided for partners. Other partners are expected to share their expectations in terms of benefits and contributions.

The partnership is more productive when it is well organized where all members have shared understanding of expectations, practices, and procedures. For example, the approach to clinical experiences in which partners will participate is best understood as the application of academic knowledge to practice. Partners participate in this process by: a) becoming familiar with the philosophy and theory undergirding the approach, and the practices, procedures, and tools for implementation; and b) providing space and support for the application of academic knowledge to practice. The reciprocal benefit for partners is through the application of academic knowledge to practice. Practitioners working directly with candidates in the teacher preparation program become familiar with new academic knowledge and its application in different settings, as well as the use of new approaches and tools related to existing knowledge. Teacher educators and candidates become aware of changes in the classroom and school environment; approaches practitioners use to address student and community needs, and state and federal mandates; and new policies and procedures required in local schools and school districts. The new knowledge of practice gained by teacher educators can be used for adjusting practices in teacher preparation. Likewise, new knowledge gained by practitioners can be used to adjust their practices and improve outcomes. Gaining this reciprocal benefit requires periodically scheduled dialogue among participants in the partnership.

It is important for participants in the partnership to understand the format for clinical experiences because of its pivotal position in the collaboration. During clinical experiences, candidates engage in observation, data gathering, documentation, analysis and interpretation of findings based on academic knowledge from coursework. This is referred to as the documented inquiry process (DIP). In their clinical experiences, candidates learn the relationship between academic knowledge and practice in different settings. Clinical experiences are guided by course assignments, key assessments, and state and national standards.

In this example, the teacher preparation program is organized into four blocks described as introductory, early, mid-level, and advanced. The content and sequence of the four blocks are based on state standards that are aligned with InTASC standards and progressions. The introductory block addresses knowledge of learners, human development, learning theory, social and cultural contexts, and learning environments. The early block is focused on English language learning, teaching and learning with technology, disciplinary literacy, content knowledge, and differentiation. The mid-level block includes assessment and data literacy, individualized instruction, and discipline specific instructional strategies. The final block is focused on application of the teaching cycle, the learning cycle, and information from the primary data collection instruments for planning and enacting learning segments.

The number of standards in each block is based on multiple factors including the time candidates' need for completing coursework and key assessments, the relationship among academic knowledge and skills across courses, and the connection of courses to specific InTASC and state standards. Specific courses, clinical experiences, and assessments located in the same block have interrelated goals and objectives.

Candidates advance through each by completing the assignments, clinical experiences, and the related key assessments. A score at the proficient level on all assessments for each block is required for advancing to the next block. All clinical experience assignments are completed individually; however, site assignments may be individual or small groups of candidates working with individual or collaborating groups of mentors. The number of candidates assigned to any school or community clinical experience site is determined by the capacity of the site as determined by practitioners at the site in collaboration with teacher educators.

All partners share information about their site and its operation in a similar format. It is important to know about the services provided, for whom, and under what conditions. The primary goals of the services, governance structure, and the regulations that enable and constrain practices within the organization are shared with partners.

Organization of Clinical Experiences

Early and mid-level clinical experiences are focused on developing professional knowledge and skills and deep understanding of the application to practice. In this approach, candidates engage in a documented inquiry process (DIP) that includes developing academic knowledge through coursework corroborated with observation, documentation, analysis, and interpretation in schools, classrooms, and communities. The interconnection between academic knowledge and teaching practice is authenticated and validated through course assignments requiring documented evidence collected in classrooms and schools. Evidence validating academic knowledge as applicable to practice is gathered through DIP. Candidates learn to use specific tools to gather information about students that will inform understanding used later in planning instruction such as the *student development inventory, student observation inventory*, and *the class profile*.

Early Clinical Experiences

Early clinical experiences are organized as clinical rounds that focus attention on specific aspects of teaching and learning (Hollins, 2015, pp. 117–134). Clinical rounds are developmentally sequenced based on the InTASC standards. The early clinical rotations are focused on diverse communities, classroom context, learner development, and the learning process. Each rotation requires the use of a specific format and tools for the documentation of observations and a written commentary.

The first clinical rotation examines the community as the context for students' growth and development outside of school. Candidates develop a community profile that includes a brief history of the development of the community; demographic composition (ethnic, racial, educational level, income, and employment sectors); governance structure, including prominent community agencies and organizations, and ethnic and racial representation and participation; and community resources related to education (schools, colleges, libraries, and historical landmarks), health (hospitals, clinics, and other agencies), and recreation (parks and recreation centers). Analysis of the demographic composition and the governance structure are aspects of understanding the culture, values, practices, and conditions in the local community. Knowledge of community resources is important for planning meaningful learning experiences that connect what students know and have experienced to academic learning in the classroom. Knowledge of health and recreation is important for referring parents and students to local agencies for meeting specific needs as necessary. Candidates develop a written commentary explaining the significance of their findings related to the community context in which students grow and develop.

The second clinical rotation examines the classroom context. Candidates use the class profile (see Table 6.1) and individual student development inventories (see Table 6.5) to analyze the social dynamic in the classroom. The classroom teacher provides the individual student development inventories from which candidates construct a class profile. Candidates focus attention on the academic, social, and psychological development of students and identify patterns of characteristics, behaviors, and social relationships based on what has been learned from coursework on child or adolescent growth and development. Candidates develop a written commentary analyzing and interpreting their observations in the classroom compared to information from the class profile and individual student inventories through the lens of knowledge from coursework.

The third clinical rotation in the early clinical experience is focused on individual learner development. In this rotation, candidates focus attention on students with specific academic, social, or psychological needs. The focus student for this rotation may be isolated or rejected by peers, struggling with academic knowledge or skills, displaying disruptive behaviors, or shy and lacking self-confidence. Candidates review the individual student inventory, make careful observations of the student in the classroom setting and interacting with students outside the classroom when

TABLE 6.1 Class profile

• Academic performance
• Differences among students
• Culture, ethnicity, social class
• Social relationships
• Social skills development
• Age, cognition, or maturity
• Peer influence (assertive, recessive)
• Interests and special talents
• Attitudes, values, perspectives
• Daily concerns
• Life experiences

The class profile indicates patterns of similarities and differences within a group of students assigned to an instructional unit or class.

possible. Candidates develop appropriate questions for interviewing the focus student based on the individual student inventory. The data on the focus student are compiled and analyzed based on academic knowledge from coursework. Candidates compile a written commentary that explains the behavior observed and propose a possible intervention based on academic knowledge.

The fourth clinical rotation in the early clinical experience addresses the learning process. Here, candidates focus attention on learning in different social arrangements, including small groups and whole class instruction. Special attention is given to the learning cycle (Figure 6.2). Candidates observe students working in small groups by first giving attention to the social dynamic in the group, including leadership and the flow of the conversation. Second, attention is given to how students understand the task, how the task is approached, and the extent to which the task is completed. Candidates are concerned with factors that facilitated or hindered task completion and each student's participation. The learning task is analyzed in relationship to the learning cycle. The commentary for completing this task integrates knowledge from the other three tasks to determine how the task in the small group work connects to what students know and have experienced outside of school; how the group assignment relates to information from the class profile and individual student inventories; and the appropriateness of the task for the developmental level of the students based on academic knowledge from coursework.

Mid-level Clinical Experiences

Mid-level clinical rotations are focused on curriculum framing, planning instruction, and assessing learning. The clinical rotations for the mid-level build upon

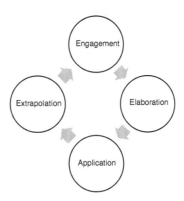

The learning cycle is a way of understanding the application of a theoretical perspective on learning, and planning and facilitating learning experiences.

FIGURE 6.1 Learning cycle

and extend knowledge from the early clinical experience. Each rotation requires the use of a specific format and tools for the documentation of observations and a written commentary.

The first clinical rotation at the mid-level is focused on curriculum framing. Curriculum framing has three parts, positioning, focusing, and contextualizing (see Figure 6.1). Candidates begin with understanding curriculum positioning. The first task in this rotation is to develop a curriculum map (see Table 6.3) for specific subject matter that integrates the structure of the discipline and common core or other state standards required by the assigned school or school district. Additionally, candidates identify the appropriate disciplinary practices for the subject matter (e.g., Next Generation Science Standards, Appendix F). The curriculum map is shared with the mentor teacher to determine where the instructional/learning segment is located and where the next segment will focus. Candidates document the conversation with the mentor teacher regarding the positioning of the curriculum.

The second task in the first mid-level clinical rotation is focusing the curriculum. The first part of this task is to determine the purpose, benefits, and outcomes for teaching and learning the specific subject matter. Here, candidates develop a statement of purpose and benefits, and develop one specific objective or learning outcome and one learning experience for a learning segment. The second part of this task is to identify the prerequisite knowledge and skills required for students to complete the learning experience and meet the learning objective.

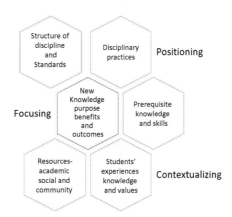

Curriculum framing is a process for making learning accessible, meaningful, and productive for students from diverse cultural and experiential backgrounds.

FIGURE 6.2 Curriculum framing

The third task in the first mid-level clinical rotation is contextualizing the curriculum. Contextualizing the curriculum connects new knowledge to students' experiences, knowledge, and values through academic, community, and social resources. Candidates review their community profiles, class profiles, and academic curriculum materials to determine which are most suitable resources for facilitating learning based on the planned learning outcomes developed in the second part of this task. Candidates write a commentary explaining the relationship among the parts of curriculum framing by referencing academic knowledge from coursework on discipline specific pedagogy and teaching students from diverse cultural and experiential backgrounds and those with special needs.

The second mid-level clinical rotation is focused on planning instruction. The task is to develop and implement a planned learning segment for a small group of students. Where candidates complete their early and mid-level clinical experiences in the same school, all work completed to this point can be used in planning instruction. This includes the community profile, class profile, individual student development inventories, curriculum map, and the curriculum framing process. Candidates work with mentor teachers to develop and implement a three-part learning segment for small group instruction. This is the candidates' first opportunity to plan a learning segment for the entire class. Candidates use the standard instructional planning format (see Table 6.2) to present their planned learning segments. The mentor teacher uses the post-observation conference format to provide feedback for the candidate.

TABLE 6.2 Standard instructional planning format

Candidate_____ Grade/subject_____ Mentor_____ Date_____   Lesson Segment Plan Subject: Content Standard: Specific Learning Objectives: Learning Experiences and Tasks: Assessment Student resources Attachments: class profile, community profile, and curriculum map

The lesson segment plan, a standard planning format, summarizes an approach for teaching a concept or skill linked to students' prior knowledge and experience that connects to future learning.

The third mid-level clinical experience is focused on the assessment of student learning. Candidates use information from their academic knowledge for developing an assessment to determine the extent to which students meet the learning objectives for the three-part learning segment. Where students fail to meet the learning objectives candidates are required to determine the cause (prerequisite knowledge or skills; connection of new knowledge with prior experiences, knowledge, or values, etc.).

Advanced Clinical Experience

Advanced clinical experience is often referred to as student teaching, an internship, or residency. Typically, student teaching is one or two semesters, and an internship or residency is one year or longer. An internship or residency can involve a full-time teaching position where the candidate is the teacher of record. Only in very rare cases is a student teacher the teacher of record. During advanced clinical practice, candidates are expected to develop and demonstrate competence in all areas of classroom teaching. This discussion addresses essential aspects of advanced clinical practice including:

- preliminary preparation,
- planning instruction,
- designing learning experiences and tasks,
- facilitating learning, and
- monitoring and assessing learner development.

Preliminary Preparation

In preparation for the advanced clinical practice, candidates are expected to compile information about the local community, the assigned school and school district, and the students in the classroom, grade level, or subject areas the candidate is assigned to teach. Information about the community includes demographic information about the population; educational and recreational resources available for children and adults; and resources available for families including health, transportation, and employment opportunities. Candidates are expected to be knowledgeable about the demographics for the school and school district, including past academic performance of students; school and district policies, practices, and curriculum standards; and school district governance. Candidates are expected to gather as much information as possible about the specific students they will teach during the advanced clinical practice period. It is important for candidates to have access to individual student development inventories for developing a class profile. Candidates are expected to have developed a community profile, curriculum map that incorporates state and/or district standards, and a class profile prior to beginning the advanced clinical practice. This information is shared with the teacher education supervisor and the mentor teacher at the beginning of the advanced clinical practice.

Planning Instruction

Planning instruction is a complex process that requires full transparency and practice for developing and demonstrating competence. This discussion addresses the protocols for making planning transparent including the curriculum map, community profile, class profile, curriculum framing, designing learning experiences, and a standard instructional planning format.

The purpose for the curriculum map is to plan instruction that supports learners in constructing a cognitive schema of interrelated and interconnected concepts and skills that form a strong foundation for increasingly complex learning, deep knowledge and understanding. The curriculum map presents the major concepts of subject matter as taught in the school curriculum. The relationship among the concepts in the curriculum map follow that of the academic discipline. The required district, state, or national standards are appropriately located within the curriculum map. A comprehensive curriculum map incorporates topics from district provided curriculum materials.

The community profile provides information about the local community that identifies the resources available for students that support their growth and development academically, socially, and psychologically. Knowledge of the community resources informs framing the curriculum and planning learning experiences for students. For example, libraries in the local community provide access to many resources for supporting the curriculum and academic learning experiences. Knowledge of education and employment patterns in the local community are indicators of the extent to which students depend on the school for their academic, social, and psychological development. This information informs the extent to which social and psychological development is incorporated into learning experiences for students.

TABLE 6.3 Curriculum map

Organizing ideas for discipline	Supporting concepts and principles	Related content standards	Discipline-specific practices	Specific learning outcomes

The curriculum map positions specific learning outcomes for a learning segment within the structure of the discipline. This supports curriculum coherence and promotes students' understanding of the interconnectedness of ideas within the discipline.

A class profile compiled from the student development inventories reveals patterns of characteristics and experiences across students. This information is essential for framing the curriculum and planning instruction. For example, knowing how many students speak English as a second language, repeated a grade level, failed a subject, or perform below grade level in basic skills inform the need for intervention or supplemental instruction. Knowledge of students' special talents and interests is equally important for planning instruction.

Curriculum framing presents a macro-level view of the mental processes, behaviors, and actions involved in planning instruction. A well-designed curriculum is the foundation for teaching. Curriculum framing is the process of making the curriculum teachable and accessible for learners. The approach to curriculum framing described in this discussion includes:

- positioning the subject matter to be learned within the structure of the discipline and employing disciplinary practices in learning experiences;
- focusing learning experiences by clearly delineating what is to be learned, purpose for learning, and the prerequisite skills required; and
- contextualizing subject matter and pedagogy based on learners' knowledge, experiences, and values supported by resources that facilitate application to practice.

Tools discussed earlier in this chapter that support curriculum framing include the community profile, class profile, curriculum map, and discipline specific pedagogy.

The information compiled for planning instruction is synthesized and applied in the planning format. The planning format consists of content standards, specific learning objectives or outcomes, learning experiences and tasks, assessment and learning resources. Some school districts require that teachers list the state or national standards addressed in the instructional plan. The specific learning objectives or outcomes are directly related to the identified state or national standards. Students' performance in relationship to the learning outcomes can be demonstrated through evidence from assessments.

Designing Learning Experiences and Tasks

The process of designing learning experiences and tasks requires deep knowledge of specific learners, learning, pedagogy, and subject matter. Designing learning experiences requires the synthesis and application of information from student development inventories, class profile, community profile, curriculum map, and curriculum framing.

Knowledge of the characteristics of individual learners, clusters of learners that share characteristics, and patterns of characteristics shared across a whole class or instructional unit informs epistemic practices, other learning experiences, and social arrangements for learning. Epistemic practices may be derived from disciplinary practices that are adapted for the specific characteristics and needs of the students being taught. For example, in using *historical inquiry* as an epistemic practice in middle school where children have limited literacy skills, video descriptions of primary source documents replace the printed text. An example at the primary school level is where children develop initial literacy skills through the *language experience* approach by dictating and learning to read their own stories, accounts of events, and letters to family and friends. The *language experience* approach is especially productive for children who speak English as a second language and for those speaking non-standard dialects of English.

The theoretical perspective on learning applied in developing learning experiences for an elementary classroom or for academic subjects in middle and secondary schools provides the coherence and continuity necessary for facilitating the development of a strong cognitive schema and deep knowledge. The preferred theoretical perspective on learning in each academic discipline is usually evident in instructional materials. Many textbooks and websites present learning experiences and tasks for teaching academic skills and subjects. Predesigned and prepackaged learning experiences require evaluation for consistency with the theoretical perspective in use, appropriateness in meeting the students' needs, and connecting with the experiences and values of the students being taught. Further, predesigned and prepackaged learning experiences require evaluation for fitting into the curriculum map and supporting the development of a strong cognitive schema for learners.

The most direct approach to developing learning experiences and tasks that include appropriate epistemic practices is the use of discipline-specific pedagogy drawn from authentic disciplinary practices. In using authentic disciplinary practices, students learn about practices in a profession or occupation, how knowledge is organized in a discipline, and how new knowledge is created, validated, and applied to practice. Further, engaging in authentic disciplinary practices is foundational for developing a strong cognitive schema to support deep knowledge and understanding within the discipline.

Facilitating Learning

Teaching and making subject matter accessible for learners is based on the quality of the curriculum framing. The positioning in the curriculum framing guides the development of cognitive schema that makes learning coherent, builds connections among ideas and academic skills, and supports memory structures that enable recall, application, and the transfer of knowledge from one context to another. Contextualizing the curriculum connects new knowledge with what learners already know, have experienced and value.

The teaching and learning cycles are macro-level views for understanding events that occur during teaching and learning. The teaching cycle illustrates the

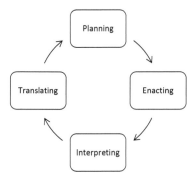

The teaching cycle involves planning instruction, enacting the plan, and observing, interpreting, and translating studentsttj responses to learning experiences for the continuous improvement of learning.

FIGURE 6.3 Teaching cycle

mental processes involved in the act of teaching. The teaching act begins with planning a learning segment. The planned learning segment is kept in mind when enacting the plan and facilitating learning. While facilitating learning, the teacher observes the learners' responses to their learning experiences. The teacher interprets the learners' responses based on knowledge of the learner, learning, pedagogy, and subject matter. These observations are translated into new actions for improving learning.

Facilitating learning begins with engaging the learner in an aspect of the curriculum that has been appropriately positioned, focused, and contextualized. Facilitating learning requires enacting the learning cycle. The learning cycle illustrates the cognitive process for developing understanding of a new concept, phenomenon, or skill. The learner is engaged with the new knowledge through experience such as conceptualization, observation, or manipulation. This engagement with new knowledge whether real, vicarious, or virtual supports the learner in generating an explanation. The learner explores the qualities of the new knowledge in relationship to prior academic knowledge and life experience. The second step in facilitating learning is elaboration that engages the learner in developing deep understanding through exploration and/or inquiry related to the analysis of the concepts, procedures, practices, and other aspects of the new knowledge that will enable application. The third step in facilitating learning is application to practice where the learner is required to develop and demonstrate understanding of conditional and procedural knowledge. The fourth step in this approach to facilitating learning is extrapolation where the learner demonstrates the ability to apply the new knowledge in a novel or unfamiliar situation.

Monitoring and Assessing Learner Development

The continuous monitoring and assessment of learner development is essential for facilitating learner growth and for developing powerful teaching practices. The depth of the assessment is influenced by the number of data points and the factors involved. The data points in this discussion include:

- student development inventories,
- class profile,
- student observation inventory,
- student performance assessment, and
- observation and documentation in logs and journals.

The factors involved in these data points are the academic, social, and psychological development of learners.

Initial assessment begins with the analysis of the student development inventory (Table 6.4) and developing the class profile. These early assessments are used in planning instruction and facilitating learning. Further, the student development inventory, the student observation inventory (see Table 6.5), and the student performance assessment are tools for monitoring and assessing individual learner progress and adjusting instruction as needed for meeting expectations for growth and development. Data from the student development inventory combined with the student observation inventory provide information for assessing social skills development, relationships with peers, and psychological development.

The purpose for assessing academic knowledge is to ensure that the depth and breadth of understanding is adequate for supporting access to increasingly complex knowledge related to what has been learned. This requires an assessment that measures more than the simple recall of information. An authentic performance assessment measures the extent to which learners can directly apply the new knowledge in appropriate situations and extrapolate the knowledge to application in novel or unfamiliar situations. Academic performance assessment is focused on the learning cycle by giving special attention to learners' ability to engage in application and extrapolation.

TABLE 6.4 Student development inventory

Student: _____
Parent: _____
Date: _____
 	
Student Development Inventory
 	
Please check any statements below that apply to you during the previous school year.
 	
  A. **Academic:**
      __ Read for pleasure regularly.
      __Traveled to a country outside the US in the past 18 months.
      __ Enjoyed the challenge of learning new skills and subject matter.
      __ Completed and submitted homework when due.

__ Struggled with basic skills in reading or mathematics.

__ Recommended for repeating the same grade (1st, 2nd, 3rd, 4th, 5th, 6th, 7th, 8th).

__ Failed one or more subjects or courses (English, math, history, science, etc.).

__ Resisted attending school.

__Changed schools one or more times during the school year.

__Speaks English as a second language.

__Special talent or skill. Please identify:_____

B. **Physical:**

__ Ate regularly scheduled and balanced meals.

__ Access to a safe place to play and exercise outside of school (yard, playground, park, etc.).

__ Regular schedule of sleep, exercise, and recreation.

__ Missed three or more days of school due to illness.

C. **Psychological:**

__Lived at home with parents and siblings.

__Lost someone or something personally important (a family member, friend, pet, etc.).

__Immigrated to the US in the past three years.

__Experienced personal trauma (illness, accident, violence, natural disaster).

__Felt sad, disappointed, preoccupied, or distracted for more than a few days.

__Felt angry, disrespected, or violated by an incident, relationship, or situation.

__Felt unsafe at home, school or other place of required attendance.

__Felt uncomfortable talking with adults (parents, teachers, counselors, administrators, etc.).

__Felt alone or isolated.

__Felt happy with the present and hopeful for the future.

__Spent more than two hours daily on the internet or playing video games.

__Engaged in activities that are age inappropriate or illegal (smoking, alcohol, drugs, sex).

D. **Social:**

__Enjoyed time with my family.

__Enjoyed attending school with my friends.

__Enjoyed time outside of school with my friends.

__Some peers were mean to me, called me names and laughed at me.

__Experienced bullying from one or more peers, in person or online.

__Actions and suggestions from teachers and administrators did not resolve my concerns.

__Parent conferences with teachers and administrators did not resolve my concerns.

TABLE 6.5 Student observation inventory

Student_____

Grade/Subject_____

Teacher_____

Date_____

Student Observation Inventory

Please check any of the statements below that apply to this student.

A. **Academic Engagement**

__Academically competent and confident.

__Shows initiative, creativity and originality.

__Completes and submits assignments when due.
__Stays focused and on task.
__Works well individually.
__Works well in small groups.
__Takes leadership role spontaneously.

B. Physical Characteristics

__Average energy level, alert, engaged.
__Low energy, slow moving, lacks stamina.
__Sleeps in class.
__Poor physical coordination.
__Poor posture.
__Taller/shorter than average for age/grade level.
__Attention getting or distracting physical attributes.
__ Neat/clean physical appearance.

C. Psychological Disposition

__Confident/self-regulation.
__Excessively gregarious.
__Shy and withdrawn.
__Impulsive/easily distracted.
__Melancholy/sad, preoccupied.
__Feels persecuted by peers and the world.

D. Social Interaction/Relationships

__Personable, outgoing, friendly.
__Well-developed social skills.
__Favored by peers.
__Isolated/rejected by peers.
__Engaged in disruptive/disrespectful behavior.

Monitoring Progress Towards Competent Teaching

Monitoring progress in achieving teaching competence is a continuous process that occurs from the beginning of the teacher preparation program to completion. Course grades are a necessary, but insufficient indicator for progress in developing the professional knowledge and skills required for competent teaching. Course grades are more reliable when course objectives or learning outcomes are linked to professional standards and course assignments provide evidence for the application of professional knowledge. For example, InTASC standard 9(j) (2013) can be applied in a course on the ethical and legal aspects of teaching as follows:

InTASC Standard 9(j): The teacher understands laws related to learners' rights and teacher responsibilities (e.g., for educational equity, appropriate education for learners with disabilities, confidentiality, privacy, appropriate treatment of learners, reporting in situations related to possible child abuse).

Course objective: Teacher candidates will analyze district and school policies and practices to determine consistency with decisions in specific Landmark Court cases, and state laws and regulations that impact teachers' and students' rights, privileges, and responsibilities.

Course assignment: Based on the readings for this segment of the course, review the policies of a local school district related to student discipline, responsibilities, and rights to determine: (a) the extent to which policies comply with court decisions, state regulations, and guidance from the US Department of education; and (b) the extent to which students' first and fourth amendment rights are protected and students receive due process when recommended for suspension or expulsion. Write a five-page paper explaining your findings. Add an appendix to your paper that includes excerpts from the policy to support your findings.

This conversion of an InTASC standard to a learning outcome is appropriate for the subject matter of the course and the course assignment supports candidates in the application of knowledge to practice by requiring a review of district and school documents for compliance with state laws and regulations. This immediate application to practice helps candidates develop the habit of mind and behaviors required for competent teaching.

A second approach to monitoring candidates' progress in developing teaching competence through understanding the application of knowledge to practice is by using an analytical journal. DIP is the core practice in this approach. Early and mid-level clinical experiences are organized around a series of carefully directed observations based on InTASC or state standards related to knowledge of learners, learning, pedagogy, curriculum framing, and classroom social context. The analytical journal incorporates a specific format of headings and discussions such as:

- event or situation observed,
- analysis and interpretation, and
- alternative approaches that might be used.

This type of journal keeping helps candidates develop an important habit of documenting and analyzing their teaching practices and observations of students' responses and behaviors. A well-designed rubric that is used across all courses is needed for evaluating journal entries. Journals can be posted to the system data base as evidence for competent teaching. Specific journal entries may be designated for individual courses.

Using key assessments is a third approach to monitoring candidates' progress in achieving teaching competence. Key assessments are a formal strategy for monitoring progress towards competent teaching where candidates engage in a predetermined set of experiences using a specific protocol for responding. Usually, key assessments address competence for pedagogical practices or discipline-specific subject matter based on standards set by state or national agencies, or professional organizations. Candidates submit responses to an electronic data base for evaluation by faculty. Candidates' performance on key assessments may require repeating one or more experiences before advancing to the next level in the program or for program completion. In some cases, completing all key assessments at the level of proficient is required for recommendation for state licensure. Key assessments are discussed more fully in Chapter 7.

Three tools are used to monitor candidates' progress in the advanced clinical practice that include pre-observation conference, post-observation conference, and observation checklist. The pre-observation conference (Table 6.6) is designed to ensure that candidates have collected appropriate information on the students they teach and the communities in which the students live; prepared a curriculum map appropriately positioning the planned sequence of learning segments; the planned learning sequence uses the appropriate format; and the planned assessment of learning outcomes adequately measures the learning goals. The observation checklist (Table 6.7) is designed to ensure that the learning segment was well planned and enacted, theoretically sound, actively engaged students, and appropriate accommodations were made as needed. The post-observation conference (Table 6.8) is aimed at supporting candidates in analyzing the results of the enacted learning segment by giving attention to learners' engagement and understanding, the need for further accommodations for specific learners, and the social relationships among learners. Each of the three tools used in monitoring progress towards competent teaching during the advanced clinical practice is based on state standards required for teacher licensure and national standards required for program accreditation. Further, the items for the post-observation conference are consistent with three of the core propositions for the National

TABLE 6.6 Pre-observation conference

Questions
1. How did you use the structure of the discipline to inform your translation of standards into specific student learning outcomes?
2. How does positioning the planned learning segment within the structure of the discipline support students' understanding of the interconnectedness of ideas?
3. How did you use information from the class profile, individual student development inventories, and individual student observation inventories in planning learning experiences.
4. How did learning theory inform the design of student learning experiences and tasks?
5. Are all learning experiences and tasks, including homework, purposefully planned to support the learning outcomes, consistent with the theoretical perspective used, and appropriately positioned within the learning cycle?
6. How will you assess students' learning and evaluate the effectiveness of the learning experiences and tasks?

The pre-observation conference is an assessment of the candidates' progress in developing a deep understanding of the complexity of the instructional planning process.

TABLE 6.7 Teaching observation checklist

Planning	
Content standards were translated into specific learning objectives for the knowledge and skills to be developed.	
The learning segment is part of a progression that follows the structure of the discipline.	
The learning experiences and tasks are well organized, clearly described and derived from the specific learning objectives.	
The learning experiences and tasks were developed based on knowledge of the specific learners, learning theory, and discipline-specific pedagogy.	
Prerequisite skills needed for the learning segment were clearly identified.	
Instruction	
Directions for the learning tasks were clearly presented in verbal and/or written language that students understood.	
Students had mastered the prerequisite skills necessary for the learning experiences and tasks.	
Students were actively engaged in the assigned learning experiences.	
Students completed all tasks as required.	
Appropriate adjustments and accommodations were made for individual students as necessary during the learning experiences and tasks.	
The candidate actively monitored students' work and provided support as necessary.	
Assessment	
The assessment adequately measured the extent to which students achieved the learning objectives.	
The same criteria are used to assess all students completing the learning experience.	
The results of the assessment provide information necessary for future planning.	

This checklist is an efficient way to focus the observation on essential aspects of competent teaching and for identifying strengths and weaknesses in examples from the candidate's teaching practices.

Board for Professional Teaching Standards: #2 teachers know the subjects they teach and how to teach those subjects to students, #3 teachers are responsible for managing and monitoring student learning, and #4 teachers think systematically about their practice and learn from experience.

TABLE 6.8 Post-observation conference

Questions
1. What observations did you make during the learning experience about students' engagement, students' level of understanding concepts and principles, and students' ability to recognize patterns and relationships among ideas in the application to practice?
2. Do some students need additional support in developing prerequisite skills or in understanding concepts and principles?
3. How do you interpret your observations regarding prerequisite knowledge and skills and students' ability to make connections?
4. What observation did you make about relationships among students and about individual participation? Do some students need additional support in developing social skills or building relationships with peers?
5. How do you explain your observations about the social dynamic during the learning experience when interpreted through the lens of adolescent or child growth and development and social skills development?
6. What adjustments or accommodations in learning experiences do you think are necessary for improving student learning outcomes and the social dynamic in the classroom?

The post-observation conference is focused on the candidate's ability to analyze students' responses to the learning experience and the social context for learning.

The pre-observation information shared with the teacher education supervisor and available for the mentor teacher includes the class profile, student development inventories, student observation inventories, community profile, three-part leaning sequence, a curriculum map, teaching log, and a brief description of the relationship among learning, learners, subject matter, pedagogy and the expected learning outcomes for the learning segment to be observed. This documentation is required for each of the five formal observations conducted by the teacher education supervisor. Mentor teachers are responsible for distributing and collecting student development inventories completed by students and parents at the beginning of the school year for most classes and each semester for others. The candidate develops the initial class profile based on student development inventories. Student observation inventories are completed by the candidate as necessary based on individual student inventories and observation of student needs during instruction. The three-part learning sequence includes one learning segment that has been taught, the learning segment that will be observed, and the next planned learning segment. This sequence demonstrates the candidate's ability to develop a sequence consistent with the curriculum map that includes interrelated concepts that develop a cognitive schema to support increasing complexity in knowledge and skills. The community profile and the class profile are the basis for connecting new learning with prior knowledge and experiences, and incorporating students' interest, value, and relevance in planning learning experiences.

The teaching journal or log documents students' responses to learning experiences and demonstrates candidates' ability to adjust instruction as necessary to improve learning outcomes.

The mentor teacher reviews each of the pre-observation artifacts at the beginning of the advanced clinical period and as new information is available. The teacher education supervisor reviews the pre-observation artifacts prior to each classroom observation. The pre-observation artifacts provide the context for the observation and for assessing the candidate's progress towards competent teaching.

During the observation, the teacher education supervisor uses the *professional practice observation checklist*, as well as personal notes, to document specific characteristics of instruction. The professional practice observation checklist consists of three parts, planning, instruction, and assessment. Much of the planning can be evaluated from the pre-observation artifacts. The application to practice in instruction is directly observed in the classroom practices. The assessment of progress towards competent teaching requires that the teacher education supervisor remains in the classroom for the complete learning segment from beginning to end during each visit. Subsequent observations are compared to the previous observation to monitor progress towards competent teaching. The five formal observations may be completed simultaneously by the mentor teacher and the teacher education supervisor or at separate times; however, the procedure is the same for both observers.

The post-observation conference is based on a series of questions to which the candidate is asked to respond in analyzing the teaching and learning experience. The questions in the post-observation conference focus on students' mastery of prerequisite knowledge and skills, understanding concepts and principles, active engagement in learning, the social context and social skills development. The questions in the post-observation conference help the candidate understand how to monitor student learning and development, and to recognize when intervention is necessary. Recognizing when students have not mastered prerequisite knowledge and skills provides opportunities for developing interventions to correct misunderstandings and gaps in knowledge and skills. Observing the extent to which students understand concepts and principles in new knowledge can reveal the need for additional support. Observations about active engagement indicate students' connection with the new content in terms of familiarity, interest, relevance, value, and understanding. Attending to the relationships among students encourages candidates to support students in need of social skills development and students who need support in accepting differences among their peers.

The mentor teacher provides consistent monitoring and support for candidates during advanced clinical practice by focusing attention on how candidates

- check for students' understanding of concepts, principles, and practices;
- adjust instruction and develop interventions for students based on individual needs; and

- attend to the social dynamic in the classroom to ensure a comfortable and supportive learning environment for all students.

The mentor teacher provides both positive feedback and suggestions.

Conclusion

The discussion in this chapter emphasized application of a clear theoretical perspective on learning to teach in designing clinical experiences. The focus for clinical experiences is described as the application of academic knowledge from coursework to practice in authentic contexts. Candidates engage in the process of learning to teach through the consistent use of specific practices, procedures and tools that support developing and demonstrating deep knowledge of the relationship among learner characteristics, learning, pedagogy, subject matter, and learning outcomes. The developmental sequence in clinical experiences is clearly delineated in three phases, early, mid-level, and advanced. The early and mid-level experiences are designed as clinical rotations with a clear focus guided by procedures and tools. The advanced clinical experience is focused on developing and demonstrating competence in all aspects of teaching. Monitoring and assessing candidates in developing teaching competence is a clearly delineated and continuous process from the early clinical experience through the advanced clinical experience.

References

American Association of Colleges of Teacher Education (2018). *A pivot toward clinical practice, its lexicon and the renewal of educator preparation.* Washington, DC: AACTE. https://secure.aacte.org/apps/rl/res_get.php?fid=3750&ref=rl.

Hollins, E. R. (Ed.) (2015). *Rethinking field experiences in preservice teacher preparation: Meeting new challenges for accountability.* New York: Routledge.

McDiarmid, G. W. & Caprino, K. (2018). *Lessons from teachers for a new era: Evidence and accountability in teacher education.* New York: Routledge.

National Council for Accreditation of Teacher Education (NCATE) Blue Ribbon Panel on Clinical Preparation and Partnerships for Improved Student Learning. (2010). *Transforming teacher education through clinical practice: A national strategy to prepare effective teachers.* Washington, DC: NCATE. http://caepnet.org/~/media/Files/caep/accreditation-resources/blue-ribbon-panel.pdf.

Next Generation Science Standards: Appendix F (2013). www.nextgenscience.org/sites/default/files/resource/files/Appendix%20F%20%20Science%20and%20Engineering%20Practices%20in%20the%20NGSS%20-%20FINAL%20060513.pdf.

Teachers for a New Era: A National Initiative to Improve the Quality of Teaching (2001). *Prospectus.* Carnegie Corporation of New York. www.carnegie.org.

7

MONITORING AND ASSESSING PROGRESS TOWARD COMPETENT TEACHING

Introduction

This chapter is focused on key assessments used as a formative assessment for the purpose of monitoring and assessing candidates' progress toward competent teaching by:

- linking coursework and clinical experiences;
- supporting candidates in developing a deep understanding of teaching and learning through observation, documentation and analysis; and
- supporting candidates in developing the habits of mind and practices that characterize competent teaching.

The key assessments are part of the structural elements that apply the conceptual elements in the program design and that support the quality indicators of coherence, continuity, consistency, and trustworthiness.

The key assessments discussed in this chapter consist of separate tasks based on each of the ten InTASC Model Core Teaching Standards (2013). Each task requires candidates to gather data (documentation, evidence, and artifacts), analyze and interpret the data, and write a commentary. The rubric is scored at four levels, unsatisfactory, basic, proficient, and distinguished. Faculty were trained and calibrated for scoring. Each completed task is scored by two faculty separately and compared for continuously monitoring interrater reliability and to ensure fairness.

Approaches to monitoring and assessing candidates' progress toward competent teaching vary across institutions and programs. Examples of approaches to monitoring candidates' progress include course grades, student teaching evaluations, video portfolios, teaching portfolios, rubrics, and course embedded assessments such as the Performance Assessment for California Teachers (PACT), an early version of the edTPA. The following discussion describes four approaches to monitoring and assessing candidates' progress, including purpose and challenges in implementation and outcomes.

Admiraal et al. (2011) conducted a study of a video portfolio used in a secondary preservice teacher preparation program for the purpose of assessing teaching competence. The approach consisted of three tasks. The first task was at the beginning of the school year and consisted of video clips of one lesson taught, the lesson plan, a reflection, and one student perspective. The second task was mid-way through the program and required the creation of several video narratives that included reflection on personal teaching qualities, video clips of teaching accompanied by lesson plans, and a narrative on methodology and practice linked to theory. The third task was at the end of the program and required a video narrative on the design, implementation, and evaluation of four lessons, two small-scale studies, video clips, and a discussion of personal teaching competence. The researchers found problems with reliability, construct validity, and consequential validity. Variations in the interpretation and evaluation of portfolio materials threatened the reliability of this assessment. Construct validity was compromised by ambiguity and inconsistency of evidence in portfolios and that a holistic assessment of teaching competence was not included. Consequential validity was compromised by the lack of transparency in teacher educators' scoring and decision making.

Wray (2007) reported a study of teaching portfolios used to assess the professional development of nine elementary candidates. Wray (2007) found that developing a portfolio assisted candidates in clarifying their instructional philosophy, better understanding the application of educational theory, and applying professional knowledge from coursework to practice. However, the challenges in using portfolios included time commitment for developing and evaluating, clarity of purpose and development process, and not all candidates benefitted equally.

Bryant, Maarouf, Burcham, and Greer (2016) reported a study on the use of a rubric for formative assessment across a teacher preparation program and as a summative assessment during student teaching. This rubric was based on the Danielson Framework for Teaching (Danielson, 2007) and the Interstate Teacher Assessment and Support Consortium (InTASC) principles (InTASC, 2013). The rubric included four domains (planning and preparation, the classroom environment, instruction, and professional responsibility) and four levels (unsatisfactory, emerging, satisfactory, and accomplished novice). The rubric was used to instruct, mentor, and assess candidates' progress toward competent teaching. The rubric was used in methods courses and field experiences across the teacher preparation program. Teacher candidates used the rubric to self-assess and reflect on specific aspects of their teaching. The researchers used confirmatory factor analysis to determine the validity and reliability of the rubric. The second version of the rubric was found to be valid and reliable for assessing candidates' competence.

Pecheone and Chung (2006) reported on the Performance Assessment for California Teachers (PACT). This assessment was designed in response to

California state legislation passed in 1998 that required a standardized performance assessment for recommending candidates for all teacher credentials. The state contracted with the Education Testing Service for developing the performance assessment made available for all programs. Any locally developed performance assessments were required to meet standards of validity and reliability. A coalition of colleges and universities formed for developing the PACT.

Pecheone and Chung (2006) stated that "the teacher performance assessment was developed as four separate and discrete performance tasks that are designed to be embedded in college or university preparation program courses" (p. 22). The PACT assessment is organized around a teaching event consisting of multiple sources of data organized into four aspects of teaching that include planning, instruction, assessment, and reflection. The multiple sources of data include teaching plans, teaching artifacts, student work samples, video clips of teaching, reflections, and commentaries. The PACT is subject specific, formative, and summative. Institutions developed embedded signature assessments for formative feedback that were shared across programs and institutions. Examples of signature assessments include case studies of individual students, instructional plans, analyses of student work, and observations of teaching. Scorers were trained and calibrated for interrater reliability. The validity and reliability of the assessment were determined through a series of carefully designed research studies.

The central purpose for key assessments, performance assessments, portfolios, and rubrics is to determine candidates' progress toward competent teaching. Each of these assessments provides data on the quality indicator of program trustworthiness. However, not all assessments of candidates' progress toward competent teaching address the program quality indicators of coherence, continuity, and consistency. The key assessments described in this chapter address candidates' progress, multiple program quality indicators, and the use of data from the assessments to improve program quality.

Purpose and Theory

The primary purpose of key assessments for the approach described in this chapter is to guide and monitor candidates in developing a deep understanding of teaching and learning through contextualizing knowledge from coursework in authentic school settings. Key assessments engage candidates in a process that:

- deepens understanding of the theory and process of learning through careful observation of students' responses to learning experiences and the social context in classrooms;
- supports developing the insight required for creating meaningful and productive learning experiences based on knowledge of learners, learning, pedagogy, and subject matter; and
- fosters the habits of mind and practices characteristic of competent teaching through routines embedded in key assessment tasks.

A constructivist theoretical perspective on learning to teach informed the development of the key assessments described in this chapter. This theoretical perspective is represented in the conceptualization of teaching as an interpretive practice/process as discussed in Chapter 3 and Chapter 6. Learning teaching using this perspective is supported by key assessments that engage candidates in:

- focused inquiry in coursework consisting of theory, research, and practice;
- directed observation involving documentation, analysis, and interpretation based on knowledge from focused inquiry; and
- guided practice based on knowledge of learners, learning, pedagogy, and subject matter.

Embedded in each key assessment is a process of data gathering, analysis and interpretation, and written commentary that supports candidates in developing the practices and habits of mind required for competent teaching. The practices of observation, documentation, and analysis are essential for developing deep knowledge for teaching in various contexts and for students with specific characteristics.

Key Assessments in Program Design

In the design of the program discussed in this chapter, key assessments are the axis for program quality indicators of coherence, continuity, consistency, and trustworthiness. The program is organized into four blocks. Each block includes interconnected courses, clinical experiences, key assessments, and specific InTASC standards. Courses, clinical experiences, and key assessments located in a specific block are linked to the same InTASC standards (see Figure 7.1 for a sample block). Courses provide academic knowledge in the form of research,

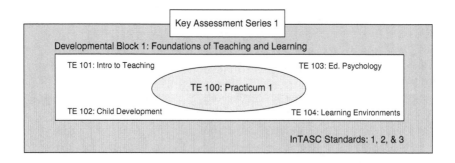

Each developmental block in a teacher preparation program consists of interconnected courses, clinical experiences, and key assessments linked to shared state and national standards translated into learning objectives related to the subject matter of each course.

FIGURE 7.1 Sample developmental block

theory, and practice. Clinical experiences provide opportunities for contextualizing and applying academic knowledge to practice. Key assessments provide the tasks that enable candidates to observe, document, and analyze the application of academic knowledge in practice.

In guiding and monitoring candidates' progress toward competent teaching, key assessments provide essential feedback on the

- sufficiency of course content and assignments,
- sequencing, cumulative progression, and increasing complexity of knowledge within and across courses, and
- consistency in the representation of the knowledge base for teaching across courses and instructors.

The trustworthiness of the knowledge base and program practices is represented in candidates' performance on key assessments, during advanced guided practice (student teaching), summative assessments, and attainment of competent teaching performance.

Monitoring and Assessment Integrated into Program Structure

Key assessments in preservice teacher preparation provide information about individual candidate readiness to move forward in a program and about aggregate program efficacy in developing candidate competency related to specific standards. The approach to program monitoring and assessment detailed in this chapter involves key assessments that are *program-embedded* as opposed to those that are *course-embedded*. In programs using either form of assessment, the knowledge base and learning experiences that prepare candidates for key assessments can be delivered in a variety of formats including courses and modules. However, program-embedded and course-embedded key assessments as described by Castle and Shaklee (2006) differ in development process, scoring procedures, and level of synthesis of professional knowledge and skill.

Castle and Shaklee's (2006) edited volume describes a course-embedded key assessment system developed by a preservice teacher preparation program in response to new NCATE (2000) requirements. In this approach, each course in the teacher preparation program designated a single assessment as part of the program assessment system. Frequently, these were pre-existing assignments or assessments that were revised with additional emphasis on validity and reliability. The course-based assessments were scored by the faculty member teaching the specific course housing the assessment, and assessment results were used both as part of course grades for individual candidates, and, in aggregate, to guide program improvement efforts.

The authors reported that advantages of such a course-based assessment system were involvement of the entire faculty in the unit assessment system and opportunity for candidates to be assessed by different faculty throughout the program. A major disadvantage was that, unless an individual assessment was weighted so heavily that failure to pass the assessment meant failure to pass the course, candidates could fail to master the competencies measured by these assessments and still be recommended for licensure. In addition, reliance on individual faculty to develop, administer, and score course-embedded assessments created challenges in maintaining the validity and reliability of the key assessments (Wei & Pecheone, 2010).

An alternative approach to course-embedded key assessments are program-embedded key assessments. Key assessments, in this case, are integral to the entire structure of the program. Each program-embedded key assessment is developed collaboratively by faculty and stakeholders across the teacher preparation program, as opposed to course-embedded assessments that are often developed by individual faculty members in isolation. This collaborative development process, described in more detail below, ensures that the key assessments as a whole represent the developmentally sequenced professional knowledge base of the teacher preparation program and reify a representation of teaching that is consistent with the program's philosophical stance and theoretical perspective. Program-embedded key assessments are also scored collaboratively by multiple program faculty, allowing for increased validity and reliability of scoring, and for shared responsibility for monitoring candidate progress and evaluating program efficacy. Program-embedded key assessments contribute to program coherence by requiring candidates to synthesize knowledge and skills across blocks of courses and clinical experiences. Program-embedded key assessments are not used to generate part of the grade of any one course.

For example, one of the key assessments for the block detailed in Figure 7.1 measures candidate ability to apply knowledge related to InTASC Standard 3: *Learning Environments*, which states that "The teacher works with others to create environments that support individual and collaborative learning, and that encourage positive social interaction, active engagement in learning, and self-motivation" (Interstate Teacher Assessment and Support Consortium, 2013, p. 8). A key assessment in that block requires candidates to gather data by observing the social interaction of students engaged in a cooperative task in their clinical experience. Candidates then analyze and interpret that data looking for patterns in group dynamics and identifying student leaders and students whose participation was limited. Finally, candidates write a commentary applying their interpretation to teaching practice by describing actions that a teacher might take to support student learning and improve student relationships in the observed learning situation.

In preparation for this assessment task, candidates engage in coursework and learning experiences related to group dynamics; classroom climate; child or adolescent development; and the observation, documentation, and analysis of evidence from the classroom. This task requires that candidates have experienced directed observation relating to each concept during the early clinical experience, with assistance from program faculty, peers, and clinical educators in connecting their observations to the professional knowledge from their coursework. In completing the key assessment task, candidates synthesize their experiences to demonstrate proficiency related to InTASC Standard 3. In succeeding blocks, candidates build upon the knowledge, skills, and habits of mind from earlier blocks. Successful completion of key assessments in each block ensures that candidates are prepared to succeed in the next block and, ultimately, in their own classrooms.

Developing Key Assessments

The key assessments described in this chapter were developed through a collaborative process where faculty reached consensus on the purpose, focus, format, position, and development. The initial discussion focused on the two principles that formed the basis for the standards set by the Council for the Accreditation of Educator Preparation (CAEP):

- Solid evidence that the provider's graduates are competent and caring educators, and
- There must be solid evidence that the provider's educator staff have the capacity to create a culture of evidence and use it to maintain and enhance the quality of the professional programs they offer.

(http://caepnet.org/standards/introduction)

The discussion on the purpose of an assessment extended beyond the CAEP requirement for candidate preparation and program effectiveness to include CAEP standards and cross-cutting themes, problems of practice identified in collaboration with partner schools, clinical experiences, other aspects of competent teaching, and the professional knowledge base (Figure 7.2). The faculty decided

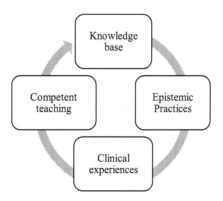

Key assessments monitor candidates progress towards competent teaching through the application of knowledge to practice in authentic clinical experiences using epistemic practices.

FIGURE 7.2 Key assessment focus

that the key assessments would address the ten InTASC standards because they subsumed state standards and are required in CAEP Standard 1.1 *Candidate knowledge and skills*. As Cogshall, Max, and Bassett (2008) argued, "In high-quality performance assessment, the criteria used to determine the quality of a teacher's performance are based on rigorous professional standards" (p. 4). A second reason for using the InTASC standards was the importance of the developmental progression indicated in faculty consensus and supported in the CAEP standards:

> 1.1 Candidates demonstrate an understanding of the 10 InTASC standards at the appropriate progression level(s) in the following categories: the learner and learning; content; instructional practice; and professional responsibility.
> *(http://caepnet.org/~/media/Files/caep/standards/caep-standards-one-pager-0219.*
> *pdf?la=en)*

The next part of designing the key assessments was to identify a specific format. The faculty agreed on a format that was consistent with the constructivist theoretical perspective and that developed the habits of mind and practices characteristic of competent teaching. The format was constructed to identify the specific InTASC standard, convert the standard to an assessment goal, and develop a task to enable candidates to meet the assessment goal for the standard (see Table 7.1). Candidates are required to gather data, analyze and interpret data, and write a commentary based on the application to practice of knowledge from coursework. This structure was congruent with the epistemic practices of learning teaching as an interpretive process (see Chapter 3)—focused inquiry, directed observation, and guided practice—reinforcing program coherence.

The faculty formed teams of two or more members to complete each task for the assessment. The first task was completed by a member of the leadership team to model the development and the faculty approval process. An initial draft of the completed task was presented to the faculty with an oral discussion of the rational, including the reason for the task, the benefit for candidates in developing teaching competence, and the expected benefit for P-12 students. The faculty asked questions and made suggestions for changes and improvements. The task planning team accepted the faculty input, revised, and resubmitted the task for approval at the next regular faculty meeting. At the faculty meeting, planning team members explained the changes made to the task. The task was approved by faculty consensus. Each task was developed and submitted to faculty for approval using this process.

When clinical experiences were organized into four blocks, the InTASC standards were developmentally sequenced across each block. A statement of purpose was written for each clinical experience block. Each course had translated appropriate InTASC standards into learning objectives with related assignments and was placed in the corresponding clinical block. Key assessments were positioned in each block.

TABLE 7.1 Key assessment format (abridged)

Title: Key Assessment 7: Planning for Instruction
Standard: InTASC Standard 7: The teacher plans instruction that supports every student in meeting rigorous learning goals by drawing upon knowledge of content areas, curriculum, cross-disciplinary skills, and pedagogy, as well as knowledge of learners and the community context.
Assessment Goals: • The teacher plans for instruction based on formative and summative assessment data, prior learner knowledge, and learner interests. • The teacher understands learning theory, human development, cultural diversity, and individual differences and the impact on ongoing planning.
Assessment Task: • Apply a specific learning theory in planning a learning experience that responds to students' interests and prior knowledge. • Develop a subject matter-specific learning experience that incorporates a cultural artifact, innovation, or act of social advocacy from an underrepresented group to illustrate a concept, principle, or skill.
Step 1: Gather data Step 2: Analyze and interpret data Step 3: Write commentary

Key assessments are based on the knowledge base for teaching and teacher preparation, state and national standards, and problems of practice in the field; and provide opportunities for candidates to demonstrate progress towards competent teaching.

The focus of each key assessment was determined by the purpose statement for the block, the associated InTASC standards, cross cutting themes, problems of practice, requirements for competent teaching, and the subject matter for the courses located in the block. The key assessment required a synthesis and application to practice of knowledge from courses in the block.

Administering Key Assessments

Candidates admitted to the teacher preparation program are provided an orientation that fully explains expectations and practices. This orientation includes a presentation of the key assessment handbook with the purpose and procedures for completing and submitting key assessments. Candidates are provided instruction for using a secure e-portfolio system, for submitting key assessments, artifacts, and supporting documents. Each candidate is assigned to a clinical experience site for completing course assignments, tasks for key assessments, and other required learning experiences. A calendar is provided with due dates for all assignments and key assessments. The calendar supports a balanced distribution of candidates' work over the semester.

Each submission for a key assessment is scored by at least two faculty. The scoring process will be more fully discussed later. Scores are made available to students through their e-portfolio accounts. Candidates do not receive individual feedback on submissions. Candidates are invited to group briefing meetings where patterns in errors and misunderstandings are discussed with examples provided. Candidates with an unsatisfactory score are referred to the university writing center for support.

The staff at the university writing center received training on the key assessments. This training included a review of the rubric, a careful examination of submissions scored at each level on the rubric, and a discussion of common errors made by candidates. When scoring has been completed for a set of submissions, a list of candidates with a score of unsatisfactory is sent to the staff at the writing center. The reason for using the writing center is that the analytical writing based on data and evidence required for key assessments is unfamiliar to many candidates.

Developing and Applying Rubrics in Scoring

Pecheone and Chung (2006) argued that performance assessments embedded within teacher education curricula are powerful because they provide evidence of program effectiveness or ineffectiveness, serve as formative instruments of candidate learning, and generate data useful for triangulating licensure decisions. In an analysis of such curriculum-embedded performance-based assessments, including observation-based assessments, on-demand performance tasks, child case studies, and portfolio assessments/teacher work sampling, Wei and Pecheone (2010) offered three criteria to evaluate strengths and weaknesses of performance assessments in teacher preparation programs:

1. How useful is the performance-based assessment for formative purposes?
2. How credible and defensible is the performance-based assessment for summative purposes?
3. How practical and feasible is the performance-based assessment? *(p. 73)*

At the core of the second criteria is the need for reliable and consistent scoring procedures, an attribute frequently found lacking in curriculum-embedded assessments in teacher preparation programs (Castle & Arends, 2006; Wei & Pecheone, 2010; Wineburg, 2006). Designing and applying appropriate rubrics for scoring key assessments is essential for developing reliable and consistent procedures, and for supporting continuous improvement and trustworthiness in teacher education programs.

Consistent with the development of the assessment tasks, the development of rubrics and scoring procedures for program-embedded key assessments is a collaborative effort. In the approach described in this chapter, a member of the leadership team created a first draft rubric for one of the key assessments. This rubric was presented to the faculty for discussion and adaptation. Once consensus was reached on language, content, and format, that rubric served as a model for rubrics to be created for other key assessments. All rubrics for the key assessments contain the same cumulative progression of required elements related to program epistemic practices. Only the holistic description on the rubric for each key assessment differs (see Table 7.2). Faculty teams responsible for drafting each key

TABLE 7.2 Sample key assessment rubric

Unsatisfactory	Basic	Proficient	Distinguished
a) The candidate did not follow the protocol for collecting student data and cultural artifact(s); **or** b) The analysis and interpretation of data were not adequate to support application to practice. *The candidate plans a learning experience without drawing upon knowledge of students, including individual interests and culture.*	a) The candidate gathered appropriate student data and cultural artifact(s); **and** b) The analysis and interpretation of data were adequate to support application to practice. *The candidate plans a learning experience based on knowledge of students, including either individual interests or culture.*	a) The candidate gathered appropriate and ample student data and cultural artifact(s); **and** b) The analysis and interpretation were adequate to support application to practice; **and** c) The candidate demonstrated the ability to apply the findings from data collection to practice. *The candidate plans a learning experience based on knowledge of students, including individual interests and culture.*	a) The candidate gathered appropriate and ample student data and cultural artifact(s); **and** b) The analysis and interpretation were adequate to support application to practice; **and** c) The candidate demonstrated the ability to apply the findings from data collection to practice; **and** d) The candidate demonstrated the ability to identify a pattern or phenomenon in the data that can be applied to other situations and identified the appropriate conditions for doing so. *The candidate plans a learning experience based on knowledge of students, including individual interests and culture, and develops cross-cultural understanding.*

This rubric follows the format for the key assessments in analyzing, interpreting, and applying findings to practice through the lens of academic knowledge.

assessment were also responsible for drafting the holistic description for the rubric. Each holistic description was presented to the faculty for consideration, revised, and approved by faculty consensus. The development of rubrics is an iterative process. Piloting assessment tasks and associated rubrics invariably reveals areas in need of improvement and adjustment in order for the assessment system to provide the data needed by faculty to monitor candidate progress and assess program efficacy (Lane & Tierney, 2008).

An essential early design decision involves establishing the structure of key assessment rubrics. Two common rubric structures are *analytic rubrics* and *holistic rubrics* (Moskal, 2001; Perlman, 2003). Analytic rubrics divide complex performance tasks into multiple distinct elements, with submissions receiving separate scores for each element. A common example of an analytic rubric is the 6+1 Trait writing rubric which is frequently used in P-12 English Language Arts instruction to rate student writing on separate elements of *ideas, organization, voice, word choice, sentence fluency, conventions,* and *presentation* (Education Northwest, 2019). In contrast, holistic rubrics provide a single rating signifying the quality of the performance inclusive of all essential task elements. Holistic rubrics emphasize the interconnectedness and integrity of task elements (Moskal, 2001). Many state-mandated standardized writing assessments use holistic rubrics for efficiency and speed in scoring (Perlman, 2003).

The key assessment approach described employs a form of holistic rubric that provides a single score indicating the level of candidate skill and knowledge demonstrated in the assessment task. However, descriptions of each level on the key assessment rubrics are cumulative and progressive. That is, to achieve a higher score, a candidate must meet all of the requirements for the lower level plus one or more additional requirements (see Table 7.2). Rubric descriptions in this approach are organized around the epistemic practices for *teaching as an interpretive process* to support program coherence. A score of *Proficient* requires that candidates demonstrate competence in gathering data (focused inquiry, directed observation) and analyzing that data for application to practice (guided practice). In addition to these indicators, each rubric includes a holistic description that informs candidates about the submission.

In drafting the initial rubrics, faculty began by describing what constitutes evidence of proficiency on a particular key assessment (Brookhart, 1999). This description was placed in the third column, *Proficient* (3), on the rubric. Additional levels on the rubric were *Unsatisfactory* (1), *Basic* (2), and *Distinguished* (4). The description of *Distinguished* included all items from the *Proficient* column plus one addition item that characterized a submission as exceeding the level of competence expected of a pre-service teacher at the point in the program when the assessment was completed. A submission scored at *Basic* fails on one item required for *Proficient*, and a submission scored *Unsatisfactory* fails on two items required to score *Proficient*.

Clear and consistent scoring procedures are essential for reliable performance assessment (Lane & Tierney, 2008). Faculty scoring key assessments were trained and calibrated in the use of key assessment rubrics. Faculty read through key assessments and associated rubrics and discussed their understanding of the tasks until they reached consensus on what each task required of candidates and what would constitute appropriate evidence. The leadership team facilitated faculty practice analyzing candidate submissions with the rubrics to develop a shared understanding of what would constitute evidence for each rubric element. Faculty scoring was considered calibrated to the rubric once 70% of scores for a single submission agreed exactly or 100% of scores were in the same or adjacent rubric columns (Stemler, 2004). However, particular attention was paid to discrepancies between faculty scoring the same submission *Proficient* and *Basic*. A submission scored *Proficient* would indicate that a candidate was making acceptable progress toward competent teaching in the area measured by the key assessment. A submission scored *Basic* required resubmission until a score of *Proficient* or above was achieved. Therefore, the decision of whether a submission was *Basic* or *Proficient* was significantly higher stakes for the candidate than differentiating between *Unacceptable* and *Basic* or between *Proficient* and *Distinguished*.

Once faculty were trained, they were assigned in dyads for scoring submissions for each key assessment. The dyads were provided blinded copies of all candidate submissions for a particular key assessment in that assessment cycle. Each member of the dyad scored all the submissions independently using the appropriate rubric. For each submission, the faculty member recorded a short explanation for the score assigned. These notes were referenced in later discussions within the dyad and with the faculty unit; and were filed for future reference as needed.

Dyad members met to compare scores. In cases where scores differed, scorers engaged in discussion until consensus was reached. If scorers were unable to reach consensus, a third reader would be invited to score the submission and facilitate discussion to reconcile scores. The faculty dyads recorded and reported each individual dyad member's initial scores and the consensus scores for every submission. The dyads also prepared a brief report for the teacher education faculty summarizing observations of patterns in candidate submissions, challenges with the structure of the assessments or the rubrics, and recommendations for action by the faculty (see Table 7.3).

Identifying Problems of Practice in Program Implementation

The primary benefit of a key assessment system such as that described in this chapter is the ability to identify problems of practice in program implementation for the purpose of continuous program improvement. Continuous program improvement requires inquiry into the discrepancy between what faculty teach and what candidates learn. Program explication and course alignment processes discussed earlier in this volume facilitate knowing what faculty teach, while a key assessment system allows for in-depth understanding of what candidates learn.

Preparing competent teachers requires a curriculum for teacher preparation that is comprehensive, cumulative, and increasingly complex. Key assessments provide

TABLE 7.3 Key assessment score report template

Submission #	Scorer 1	Scorer 2	Consensus Score	Comments
Candidate 1				
Candidate 2				
Candidate 3				
Candidate 4				
Candidate 5				
Report to Faculty (observed patterns in candidate submissions; challenges in task or rubric format; recommendations for action):				

Tracking individual and consensus scores is required for maintaining consistency and reliability in scoring and using data from submissions for continuous program improvement.

an indication of the integrity of the conceptual and structural elements of the program. The sequencing of key assessments throughout the program allows faculty to determine if the courses and clinical experiences in each block of the program are effective in facilitating candidates' ability to apply the knowledge base to practice. Opportunities for intervention occur when an individual candidate performs poorly on a particular key assessment. When several candidates perform poorly on a specific key assessment, the faculty investigate to determine what factors in the program might be adjusted to better facilitate progress towards competent teaching.

If candidates in a program consistently score lower on a particular key assessment than on others, the faculty has evidence that either the assessment needs adjustment or that the program coursework has not fully prepared candidates to apply to practice the professional knowledge on which the assessment is based. Focus groups with candidates who have completed the assessment and faculty collaboration using candidate submissions and completed assignments from coursework support identifying areas of weakness. If the problem is within the assessment, faculty can collaborate to develop tools and scaffolds to help candidates better understand what is required. Possible scaffolds include, but are not limited to, glossaries, data collection organizers, and more detailed instructions. If the problem is not in the assessment, but rather is a manifestation of candidates' misunderstanding some aspect of the knowledge base or its application to practice, then faculty collaboration is focused on adjusting coursework and clinical experiences to improve candidate preparation in that area. Faculty investigate the specific course objectives related to that aspect of the knowledge base, the course assignments, and associated resources to determine adequacy for the application of academic knowledge to practice and for supporting progress towards competent teaching (see Chapter 5 for description of a course alignment process to support this inquiry). When gaps in knowledge or experience are identified, faculty collaborate to adjust the knowledge base and learning experiences to address the pattern(s) of misunderstanding or inappropriate application observed in candidate submissions.

Conclusion

This chapter emphasizes the importance of a program-embedded key assessment system to monitor candidates' progress toward competent teaching and facilitate improvement of program quality based on relevant data. Key assessments and associated rubrics and scoring procedures are collaboratively designed by faculty and stakeholders. Employing the program-embedded key assessment system described in this chapter, paired with the explication and alignment processes discussed in Chapters 4 and 5, and the clinical experience structure described in Chapter 6, leads to preservice teacher preparation program design characterized by coherence, continuity, consistency, and trustworthiness.

References

Admiraal, W., Hoeksma, M., van de Camp, M., & van Duin, G. (2011). Assessment of teacher competence using video portfolios: Reliability, construct validity, and consequential validity. *Teaching and Teacher Education, 27,* 1019–1028.

Brookhart, S. M. (1999). The art and science of classroom assessment. The missing part of pedagogy. *ASHE-ERIC Higher Education Report, 27* (1).

Bryant, C. L., Maarouf, S., Burcham, J., & Greer, D. (2016). The examination of a teacher candidate assessment rubric: A confirmatory analysis. *Teaching and Teacher Education, 57,* 79–96.

Castle, S. & Arends, R. (2006). Developing credible performance assessments. In S. Castle & B. D. Shaklee (Eds.), *Assessing teacher performance: Performance-based assessments in teacher education* (pp. 35–48). Lanham, MD: Rowman & Littlefield.

Castle, S. & Shaklee, B. D. (2006). *Assessing teacher performance: Performance-based assessment in teacher education.* Lanham, MD: Rowman & Littlefield.

Coggshall, J., Max, J., & Bassett, K. (2008). Key issue: Using performance-based assessment to identify and support high-quality teachers. http://eric.ed.gov/?id=ED543665.

Danielson, C. (2007). *Danielson's framework for teaching.* Washington, DC: ASCD.

Education Northwest (2019). 6+1 trait rubrics. https://educationnorthwest.org/traits/traits-rubrics.

Interstate Teacher Assessment and Support Consortium (2013). *InTASC model core teaching standards and learning progressions for teachers.* Washington, DC: Council of Chief State School Officers.

Lane, S. & Tierney, S. T. (2008). Performance assessment. In T. L. Good (Ed.), *21st century education: A reference handbook.* Thousand Oaks, CA: Sage Publications.

Moskal, B. M. (2001). Scoring rubrics: What, when and how? *Practical Assessment, Research and Evaluation*, 7 (3), 1–5.

National Council for the Accreditation of Teacher Preparation (NCATE) (2000). *Professional standards for the accreditation of teacher preparation institutions.* Washington, DC: Author.

Pecheone, R. L. & Chung, R. R. (2006). Evidence in teacher education: The Performance Assessment for California Teachers (PACT). *Journal of Teacher Education*, 57 (1), 22–36.

Perlman, C. (2003). Performance assessment: Designing appropriate performance tasks and scoring rubrics. In J. E. Wall & G. R. Walz, *Measuring up: Assessment issues for teachers, counselors, and administrators* (pp. 497–506). Greensboro, NC: CAPS Press.

Stemler, S. E. (2004). A comparison of consensus, consistency, and measurement approaches to estimating interrater reliability. *Practical Assessment, Research & Evaluation*, 9 (4). https://scholarworks.umass.edu/pare/vol9/iss1/4/.

Townsend, B. K. & Ignash, J. M. (2003). Community college roles in teacher education: Current approaches and future possibilities. *New Directions for Community Colleges*, 121, 5–16.

Wei, R. C. & Pecheone, R. L. (2010). Assessment for learning in preservice teacher education. In M. Kennedy (Ed.), *Teacher assessment and the quest for teacher quality: A handbook* (pp. 69–132). San Francisco, CA: Jossey-Bass.

Wineburg, M. (2006). Evidence in teacher preparation: Establishing a framework for accountability. *Journal of Teacher Education*, 57 (1), 51–64.

Wray, S. (2007). Teaching portfolios, community, and preservice teachers' professional development. *Teaching and Teacher Education*, 23, 1139–1152.

8

RESPONDING TO NEEDS, MANDATES, AND STANDARDS

Introduction

This chapter is focused on the interconnectedness of local community and school needs, state and national standards for P-12 education, and teacher preparation. This chapter has three parts that include assessing and responding to local needs, responding to state mandates and standards, and responding to national standards and accreditation requirements. Emphasis is placed on improving P-12 education for the common good and public interest as the overarching purpose for mandates, regulations, and standards imposed on public schools and teacher preparation at the state and national levels. The interconnectedness and singular purpose of state and national mandates provide opportunities for teacher educators to develop responses that simultaneously meet multi-level expectations while focusing on the central purpose of improving P-12 student learning and development through teacher preparation.

The impact of P-12 education on the quality of life for individuals and in communities provides compelling evidence for attention and action by education providers, stakeholders, and at all levels of government. Data from the National Center for Educational Statistics indicates that educational attainment influences most other quality of life indicators in the society (Hussar et al., 2020). The quality of the curriculum and pedagogy in P-12 schools has a primary impact on students' academic performance and subsequent educational attainment. For example, the fact that 57% of entering college freshmen need remediation in English language arts and mathematics indicates problems with the curriculum and pedagogy in P-12 schools (Barry & Dannenberg, 2016; Jimenez, Sargrad, Morales, & Thompson, 2016).

Further, data from the National Center for Educational Statistics (McFarland et al., 2019) indicate that educational attainment is associated with annual earnings.

These data reveal that full time employed young adults ages 25–34 with a high school diploma had median annual earnings of $32,000, with a bachelor's degree $52,000, and with a master's degree or higher $65,000. Young adults with less than high school completion had higher rates of unemployment and poverty. These data suggest that low-performing schools and underperforming teachers contribute to poverty in low-income communities and to shortages in employment sectors requiring specialized skills in mathematics and science. Low performing urban schools are an issue to be addressed by both local school districts and teacher preparation program providers.

The underperformance of students in P-12 schools and the impact on further educational attainment are decades-old persistent problems related to the school curriculum, teaching practices, and the professional knowledge base. These issues require attention from teacher educators and stakeholders in examining the adequacy of teaching practices, subject matter knowledge for teaching, the professional knowledge base for teaching, and clinical experiences provided for candidates learning to teach. The interrelatedness of P-12 student development, teaching, and teacher preparation is evident in local schools. Productive responses to these issues require attention to local needs.

Assessing and Responding to Local Needs

Assessing and responding to local needs are essential for productive collaboration among teacher educators, practitioners, and stakeholders focused on improving P-12 student learning outcomes and teacher preparation program development and renewal. Indicators of local needs directly related to teaching and teacher preparation include school performance, high school graduation rates, educational attainment beyond high school, and employment rates and sectors. Underperformance in any of these areas requires research into the relationship to the school curriculum and pedagogy. For example, situations where specific subgroups are underperforming in areas such as language arts and mathematics raise questions about the framing and contextualizing of the curriculum and pedagogy for students from different cultural and experiential backgrounds (see Chapter 6). Students who struggle with basic skills in P-12 schools are less likely to continue their education beyond high school.

Many factors in low income and urban communities influence students' access and opportunities for learning and their availability for full participation in learning experiences. These factors include culture and language, family income and resources, relocation, and living arrangement. Culture and language differences can contribute to communication barriers between parents and children, and between families and school practitioners. Many parents work two or more jobs to provide food, shelter, and other necessities for their families, which limits the time available for the nurturing, guidance, and support needed for children's academic, psychological, and social development. Families may not have financial resources for materials and tools for learning, including technology. Children and families are often displaced by natural disaster, placement in foster care, homelessness, relocation, or immigration. These experiences are real. However, children have other experiences in their communities where they interact with other children and adults in different contexts and social gathering that are recreational, educational, and religious. Families and children make use of local services and resources in the community including medical facilities, social services, parks, historical sites, recreational facilities, museums, shops, restaurants, and churches. It is important for teachers and teacher educators to be familiar with the experiences, challenges, and resources in the local community (Hollins, 2012, 2019).

The conditions in local communities have implications for adjustments in the knowledge base for teaching and the related clinical experiences for the application of academic knowledge to practice. These adjustments to the knowledge base for teaching influence the framing and content in all five areas—learners, learning, pedagogy, subject matter, and context. Context is the central organizing factor in the knowledge base (Chapter 4). The local community where children are socialized is the place for candidates to learn the application of academic knowledge to practice for local children. The experiences children have in their homes and local community constitute the context through which they learn to make sense of the world. Candidates learn to make connections with how children make sense of the world for planning meaningful and productive learning experiences. This requires that the knowledge base for teaching include research, theory, and practice that support candidates' understanding in this area. Another example is knowing that many children living in poverty may not have their parents available for important aspects of guidance that supports social and psychological development, requires that candidates learn to support children in developing social skills and self-regulation, rather than focusing on classroom control and punitive discipline. Candidates need opportunities to make observations in classrooms serving students from diverse cultural and experiential backgrounds where they can apply teaching practices that fully support children's growth and development.

Candidates benefit from clinical experiences located in schools with students from diverse cultural and experiential backgrounds that provide opportunities for observing learning challenges and successes. In these situations, candidates analyze students' learning experiences to determine the effectiveness of specific pedagogical practices and curriculum framing—positioning, focusing, and contextualizing (Chapter 6). This type of clinical experience enables candidates to deepen their understanding of the relationship among learner characteristics, learning, pedagogy, subject matter, and learning outcomes.

Assessing Competence for Teaching Underserved Students

Assessing competence for teaching underserved students is a challenge for school practitioners and teacher educators. School practitioners need the ability to identify the specific academic knowledge and its application to practice that enables effective teaching for traditionally underserved students. This will enable school practitioners to recruit and recognize novice and experienced teachers with the professional knowledge and skills for fostering high academic performance for traditionally underserved students. Teacher educators need to design teacher preparation programs that include conceptual elements that inform the selection, admission, and preparation of candidates with the knowledge and skills for teaching traditionally underserved students. Teacher recruitment for underperforming schools begins with the admission of candidates into teacher preparation programs. Teacher educators create the pool of licensed teachers from which school practitioners recruit. Ethical practices for the profession demand that teacher educators recommend only those candidates who demonstrate competence for teaching students from diverse cultural and experiential backgrounds to meet expectations for the subject matter and grade level for which they will be licensed. Occasionally, a candidate will appear to demonstrate the appropriate teaching competence during preparation; but will be unable to perform as a novice teacher charged with facilitating learning. In such cases, school practitioners need to be knowledgeable about assessing teaching practices, providing interventions, and removing from employment as appropriate.

Promising Practices

Chapter 6 provides tools for guided practice during advanced clinical experiences in a teacher preparation program. These tools include pre-and post-observation protocols and an observation checklist. These practices monitor and assess candidates' progress towards competent teaching. The focus is on the application of academic knowledge to practice, P-12 students' responses to learning experiences, the assessment of student learning, and adjusting teaching practices as necessary to improve learning outcomes. This approach to monitoring progress towards competent teaching provides information for supporting candidates in the application of academic knowledge to practice and informs teacher educators of the need for adjusting the knowledge base for teaching and clinical experiences in teacher preparation. Improvements in the preparation of candidates strengthens the professional pool from which practitioners select and hire classroom teachers.

When recruiting teachers for urban schools, attention to applicants' responses to the following questions can provide insight into their potential for facilitating meaningful and productive learning experiences:

- How would you approach a situation in an urban school where you need to determine the extent to which students are prepared for grade level curriculum and learning experiences?
- If you determined that 50% or more of your students perform several years below grade level in reading and mathematics, what strategies would you use

to improve their basic skills and provide access to grade level curriculum and learning experiences?

- How would you develop a classroom environment that is engaging, motivating, and supportive for students who have experienced trauma and disappointment in their daily lives outside of school and anxiety and frustration academically, emotionally, and socially inside school?

Appropriate answers to these questions are related to knowledge and experiences in advanced clinical practice in Chapter 6. Teacher applicants are expected to respond with academic knowledge related to child and adolescent growth and development, the identification and assessment of prerequisite knowledge and skills for the subject matter being taught, and curriculum framing—positioning, focusing, and contextualizing. Applicants unable to respond appropriately to these questions require additional preparation to be successful in facilitating learning for underperforming urban students.

Teaching students who have been traditionally underserved and have not had access to high quality learning experiences requires detailed planning that is labor intensive and time consuming. Teachers who develop the expertise, invest the time and effort, and whose students achieve or make significant progress towards grade level and subject matter expectations deserve appropriate recognition and reward. Research shows that this is often not the case (New Teacher Project, 2012).

Improving Teaching Practices in Underperforming Schools

Underperforming schools and students are a challenge for school practitioners and teacher educators. Practitioners need to identify approaches for selecting teachers who foster high outcomes for students in critical areas or to develop approaches for professional development that consistently improve teaching practices. Teacher educators need to identify or develop approaches that enable candidates to consistently use their knowledge of *teaching as an interpretive practice* to address problems in the alignment of learner characteristics, learning, pedagogy, subject matter, and learning outcomes. Candidates need to take from their teacher preparation programs an approach for continuously improving teaching practices that is sustainable and that fosters collaboration among colleagues. Such an approach will support novice teachers and their students in achieving the expected learning outcomes for the subject matter and grade level.

Promising Practices

Hollins (2006, 2012) identified an approach for the continuous improvement of teaching practices in early literacy development referred to as *structured dialogue.*

This approach was first studied in urban elementary schools in California and Ohio with early literacy and later in secondary science in an urban high school in California (Linton, 2011). The consistent use of this approach generated similar positive results in each setting.

The approach required that each teacher keep a journal documenting teaching practices and students' responses, meeting for one hour each week using structured dialogue, and keeping a record of decisions made by the group that was available to participants. During the one-hour weekly meeting, each participant shared one success and one challenge that included students' responses. After all participants had shared their experiences, questions were asked to clarify teaching practices and students' responses. The group identified challenges or issues that were shared among several participants and developed an agreed upon strategy that all would implement. Each meeting used the same format for sharing experiences. Progress with agreed upon strategies was discussed at subsequent meetings. The teacher leader selected by the group kept the group focused and monitored the time.

The benefit for teachers using structured dialogue consistently included:

- access to knowledge distributed across the group;
- awareness that not all teachers shared the same challenges;
- deeper understanding of the relationship among learner characteristics, learning, pedagogy, subject matter, and learning outcomes; and
- shift in perspective from blaming failure on students' ability and effort to accepting responsibility for learning outcomes based on teaching practices.

The sustainability of student learning gains and the continuous improvement of teaching practices in this case is embedded in the consistent use of structured dialogue and the documentation of practice.

Drawing on Hollins (2006, 2012) work on structured dialogue, Warner and Hallman's (2017) study of mid-level clinical experiences in preservice teacher preparation, described an approach to clinical experience that implemented structured dialogue between candidates, mentor teachers, and university supervisors. Structured dialogue based on problems of practice within the clinical site shifted the locus of conversation in the clinical experience triad from candidate performance or approximation of the mentor teacher's practice to P-12 student response to learning experiences. This approach served as a professional learning activity that generated improved practice within partner schools and contributed to the collaborative skills and abilities of all parties involved. The goal of this approach was to develop a community of practice inclusive of parties in both the university and the clinical site. Structured dialogue is an example of one well documented approach that can be implemented by practitioners and teacher educators that has the power and sustainability for improving learning outcomes in many school settings.

Addressing Problems beyond the Authority of Teacher Educators

Many problems of practice in P-12 schools are beyond the authority and responsibility of teacher educators, such as those resulting from decisions in local school districts made by district administrators and school boards. For example, school districts select and adopt textbooks, mandate specific teaching practices, set policies for students to repeat subjects and grade levels, and often do not engage in the research necessary for determining the impact of such decisions. Changes in the curriculum adopted by school districts can be influenced by the preferences of new administrative leadership without consideration for student characteristics or what is presently effective or ineffective. Decisions about curriculum and pedagogy can be influenced by the values and preferences of school principals, central office administrators, or a single charismatic motivational speaker. These values and preferences are often evident in teacher evaluations. Teachers frequently complain that professional development for new curriculum or pedagogical approaches is inadequate. The context for teaching in some school districts makes it difficult for novice teachers to apply the academic knowledge from teacher preparation.

Promising Practices

A major challenge for teacher educators is addressing problems of practice in schools and school districts that are outside their authority and responsibility. One approach to addressing such challenges is incorporating collaborative practice-based research and decision making into partnership agreements. This requires that such agreements clearly state the process for identifying issues and problems most in need of investigation, the approval process, and the necessary arrangements and resources. Such an agreement has reciprocal benefits for informing and improving school practices and teacher preparation.

Practice-based research can be used to address many different areas including:

- the impact of specific teaching practices on the persistent underperformance of traditionally underserved groups in specific academic skills and subject matter areas;
- the impact of curriculum changes in critical areas such as literacy, mathematics, and science;
- the impact of specific policies such as repeating a grade level or subject on subsequent learning; and
- the impact of specific policies and practices on the social context in schools and classrooms.

The type of practice-based research discussed here investigates teaching practices, student learning, and the social context in classrooms and schools. For example, research on academic learning examines:

- the alignment among learner characteristics, learning, pedagogy, subject matter, and learning outcomes;
- curriculum framing—positioning, focusing, and contextualizing; and
- the application of learning cycles and teaching cycles.

This type of research requires examination of teachers' documentation of their practices and students' responses, lesson plans extending over several weeks, and samples of students' work. Such research is expected to identify problems in the curriculum, pedagogy, learning experiences, and instructional materials. Some approaches and instructional materials may be found more appropriate for one group of students and not others. Research on the social context in the classroom examines the relationship between the teacher and the students and among students. These studies determine if students feel accepted, comfortable, connected, and supported. Such studies are expected to identify students in need of social skills development, support in developing self-regulation, and those with other social and psychological needs that are unmet.

Practice-based research requires gaining a deep understanding of the problem or issue within the context of existing conditions and practices prior to making recommendations for adjustments or changes. This is not an opportunity for teacher educators to implement their personal preferences for instructional approaches or to frame research studies to pursue their unique personal interests. Practice-based research serves the interest of local schools, students, and communities. Teacher educators engaged in practice-based research need to have the appropriate expertise for the issues and problems addressed.

Practice-based research follows all standards and protocols required by universities and school districts, including approval by the Institutional Review Board (IRB) for each institution. IRB approval needs to include permission for publication in the scholarly literature for the advancement of the profession. Research conducted for the benefit of schools and school districts requires a written research report submitted to the district administrators and discussions as requested.

Practice-based research has benefits and costs. This research can support schools and school districts in improving the conditions, quality, and outcomes of schooling for students. It can provide valuable information used to improve teacher preparation and professional development. These benefits are shared by school districts and teacher preparation providers. Likewise, the cost needs to be shared by the institutions benefitting from the research. For example, teacher educators and school practitioners often need time release from their regular duties to engage in such research. There are costs associated with data gathering and analysis. These costs can be covered through shared budgeting or grant funding. The value of this type of collaborative research is far greater than the cost. Practice-based research assists teacher educators and practitioners in meeting local needs for improving teaching and teacher preparation, and in meeting state mandates and standards.

Responding to State Mandates and Standards

State legislative initiatives and mandates for education are intended to improve the quality of education available for residents and the quality of life in communities. A central concern is the influence of education on the economy. Many teacher educators and school practitioners resent discussion of the connection between public education and the economy. However, parents need employment and a living wage income to provide a reasonable quality of life for their children. The Education Commission of the States has focused its attention on the connection between education and the workforce (Ujifusa, 2019). In 2018, state lawmakers introduced 165 bills addressing the link between education and the workforce; 27 bills became law. Attention has focused on the quality of education in general and on shortages in specific sectors of the workforce that impact the economy. Attracting large corporations to locate in a state is influenced by the availability of a workforce with the appropriate knowledge and skills. The failure to attract large corporations can devastate the state economy and increase unemployment and poverty. State regulation of teacher preparation is directly linked to the quality of education provided in P-12 schools and the state economy.

States set standards for teacher preparation programs, assessment of candidates, curriculum standards for P-12 schools, P-12 student assessment, and requirements for high school completion. These different levels of knowledge and assessments related to P-12 education are interconnected and interdependent. The quality of education available in P-12 schools is significantly influenced by the quality of the school curriculum, the knowledge base for teaching and teacher preparation, and clinical experiences provided for candidates. The expectation is that the subject matter preparation for teachers aligns with the curriculum at the grade levels for which candidates will be certified or licensed to teach, and that the professional knowledge base for teaching and teacher preparation includes the appropriate discipline specific pedagogy and other teaching practices. The state assessments for P-12 students and for the licensure of candidates are intended to ensure that each meet expectations for knowledge, skills, and performance.

A major contributing factor to low academic performance among P-12 students and low-performing schools is the misalignment of teacher preparation with the expectations and needs in P-12 schools. State departments of education have sought to correct this misalignment through mandates and regulations for P-12 education and teacher preparation. Examples of these attempts at correction include the Common Core State Standards for P-12 schools and new teacher performance assessments and discipline specific tests for teacher licensure. The states have collaborated with each other through the Council of Chief State School Officers and collectively with the United States Department of Education on policies and regulations for teacher preparation.

Presently, states are faced with teacher shortages in mathematics, science, special education, English learners, career and technical education, and in urban and rural schools. How states respond to such shortages has the potential of long-term effects for individuals and communities across the nation. In some instances, states are responding by lowering standards for teacher preparation and teacher licensure and increasing the authorization for temporary and emergency licensure in areas of teacher shortages. In a policy brief for the Education Commission for the States it was argued that:

> The certification route new teachers choose does not appear to have a significant effect on teaching quality, nor does teaching quality vary much between types of certification program applicants. Teacher effectiveness is similar across programs with low and high coursework requirements and across highly selective or less selective programs. Additionally, research has found no distinction between alternatively and traditionally certified teachers as far as their "scores on college entrance exams, the selectivity of the college that awarded their bachelor's degree or their level of educational attainment."
>
> *(Woods, 2016)*

This argument is based on two reports from the Institute for Education Sciences (IES) and one report from the National Council of Teacher Quality (Greenberg, Walsh, & McKee, 2014). The first IES report is on teachers trained through different routes for certification (Constantine, Player, Silva, & Hallgren, 2009) and the second is on teacher shortages in schools serving disadvantaged students (Institute of Education Sciences, 2013). The report from the National Council of Teacher Quality (NCTQ) is a review of teacher preparation programs. The central issue in teacher preparation of *continuously reproducing existing teaching practices and learning outcomes* through a cognitive apprenticeship approach in clinical experiences and in mentoring novice teachers is not addressed in these reports or in other recommendations for addressing teacher shortages that we reviewed.

For example, the Southern Regional Education Board (SREB), Teacher Preparation Commission (December 2018), identified the following promising practices for improving teacher preparation with a focus on addressing teacher shortages:

1. Hold all new teachers in a state to the same high standards, and require candidates to demonstrate mastery of practical classroom skills through practice-based licensure tests.
2. Require high-quality clinical teaching experiences.
3. Develop comprehensive statewide data systems for continuous improvement.
4. Encourage strong partnerships between teacher preparation programs and K-12 districts.

The Learning Policy Institute recommends "a comprehensive and systematic set of strategies to build a strong, stable profession, as was done in medicine more than half a century ago" (p. 70). This includes:

- Creating competitive and equitable compensation packages that make teaching an affordable choice for candidates across communities.
- Enhancing the supply of qualified teachers targeted to high-need fields and locations through targeted training subsidies and high-retention pathways.
- Improving teacher retention, especially in hard-to-staff schools, through improved mentoring, induction, working conditions, and career development.
- Developing a national teacher supply market, with license reciprocity and portable pensions that can facilitate getting and keeping teachers in the places they are needed over the course of their careers.

(Sutcher, Darling-Hammond, & Carver-Thomas, 2016)

These policy proposals and practices are useful and important. However, they do not address the basic challenges in teacher preparation program design or traditional practices for mentoring novice teachers. Three central challenges in teacher preparation discussed across the chapters in this book include:

- instability in the knowledge base for teaching and teacher preparation,
- disassociation of the knowledge base from the application to practice in clinical experiences, and
- the use of a cognitive apprenticeship approach to clinical experiences that continuously reproduces existing teaching practices and learning outcomes.

These challenges exist across many teacher preparation programs including those that are traditional, alternative, or residency regardless of location, type of institutional affiliation, and other conditions. Traditional practices for mentoring novice teachers employ a cognitive apprenticeship approach with similar results of reproducing existing teaching practices and learning outcomes. Improving the effectiveness of teacher preparation and student learning outcomes requires, at a minimum, addressing the three central challenges described here and across the chapters in this book. This discussion has important implications for policies and practices related to program accreditation and licensure standards intended to improve student learning outcomes and to address teacher shortages.

Teacher Preparation Programs and Licensure Standards

The Council of Chief State School Officers (CCSSO) first convened in 1908 to advise the United States Congress on issues related to vocational education. During the 1960s the group advocated for the Elementary and Secondary

Education Act and began an alliance with the United States Department of Education to provide advice on education policies. In 1987 CCSSO formed the Interstate New Teacher Assessment and Support Consortium (INTASC) comprised of state education agencies responsible for teacher licensure, program approval, and teacher development. This group was charged with developing the following (CCSSO, 2016):

- Compatible educational policy on teaching among the states
- New accountability requirements for teacher preparation programs
- New techniques to assess the performance of teachers for licensing and evaluation
- New programs to enhance the professional development of teachers.

Major accomplishments for INTASC include the following:

- Development of the model "core" standards for beginning teachers
- Translated model core standards into model licensure standards for specific subject matter specializations
- Developed the initial new licensing examinations
- Developed and validated model performance assessments using candidate portfolios
- Developed principles for quality teacher preparation programs
- Provided consultation for states in the implementation of standards-based licensing systems.

Each state develops or approves standards and regulations for teacher preparation and the evaluation of teaching. The INTASC standards and progressions have significant influence.

State authorization and approval are required for programs that prepare teachers for licensure. Program authorization and approval are based on a set of standards determined by state education agencies. The process of program authorization and approval include examining multiple sources of evidence and conducting site visits to evaluate the extent to which teacher preparation programs meet the required standards, conducting joint site visits with a national accreditation agency, or accepting the findings and recommendations based on evaluations conducted by a national accreditation agency.

State standards and requirements for teacher preparation programs and teacher licensure are more detailed and specific than those set by national accreditation agencies, but tend to require less detailed evidence. State standards limit the number of courses in teacher preparation programs, change course requirements, determine the conditions for clinical experiences and the qualifications for mentor teachers. State standards are developed and changed in response to the academic performance of P-12 students, other conditions in public schools, and the educational needs across the state.

Understanding the impetus for changes in state standards and requirements for teacher licensure and the authorization and approval of teacher preparation programs is essential for responding in ways appropriate for meeting expectations and societal needs. This requires more than adding and deleting courses, locating courses in school buildings, and increasing the number of hours in clinical experiences. Meeting new expectations requires:

- careful examination of the conditions in public schools related to learning outcomes and the social context;
- the impact of P-12 education on college entrance and the workforce; and
- the alignment between teaching and teacher preparation.

Each new mandate needs to be carefully examined and the options for meeting expectations clearly delineated.

Developing a credible response to changes in state requirements demands careful examination of data on student academic performance in basic skills and academic subjects, high school completion rates, college entrance and completion rates, and reports on supply and demands in specific employment sectors across the state. These data can provide useful information on possible weaknesses in teachers' subject matter knowledge, pedagogical content knowledge, or understanding of curriculum framing. Surveys of employer and program completer satisfaction provide valuable information on possible areas of weakness in teaching performance based on limitations in the knowledge base or clinical experiences. Adjustments in teacher preparation cannot address all the problems of practice in teaching and P-12 learning outcomes as discussed earlier; but can contribute to improving school and classroom practices.

Mandated Assessments for Teacher Licensure

The National Assessment of Educational Progress (NAEP) for students began in 1969. The purpose was to assess what students know and can do in core academic subjects. In 1988 Congress authorized the trial state assessments that were conducted in 1990, 1992, 1994. In 1996 these assessments became routine. The 2001 Reauthorization of the Elementary and Secondary Education Act required that states receiving Title I funds participate in NAEP testing at Grades 4 and 8 every two years. The NAEP assessment at this point addressed subject matter performance, instructional experiences, and school environment by grade level and subgroups. The intent of these assessments was to identify strengths and weaknesses in student academic performance and related school practices with expectations for improvement. Many school practitioners responded by narrowing and fragmenting the school curriculum and engaging students in rote learning to improve student performance on the NAEP and other assessments of students' academic performance, rather than working to improve classroom instruction and student learning. Very little improvement in student learning has resulted from these practices.

Student underperformance in elementary and secondary schools has resulted in a high percentage of entering college freshmen requiring remediation in English language arts and mathematics. Candidates for teacher preparation are selected from among this pool of entering college freshmen. In many cases, remediation does not fully correct the gaps in academic knowledge and skills resulting from underperformance in elementary and secondary schools. This creates the potential for a cycle of mediocrity (Figure 8.1). In attempting to disrupt this cycle, policymakers instituted a series of teacher tests as measures of readiness for teaching that are required for state licensure. Many teacher educators and candidates argue that such tests do not measure the potential for effective classroom teaching, instead, they arbitrarily prevent otherwise well qualified teachers from entering the profession. The claim further suggests that many who fail such tests are as qualified as those who pass. Many individuals making such arguments have few viable suggestions for ways to improve teaching practices and learning outcomes for students in P-12 schools.

Presently, most states have three levels of candidate assessment for licensure that address basic skills, subject matter knowledge, and professional knowledge and skills for teaching. Candidates are required to achieve a predetermined passing score on each test to qualify for licensure. Examples of the three levels of testing for the state of California include the California Basic Educational Skills Test

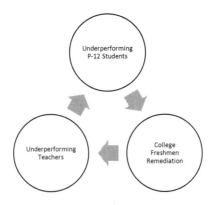

Disrupting the cycle of mediocrity is a major challenge for teacher educators in designing the knowledge base for teaching and teacher preparation.

FIGURE 8.1 Cycle of mediocrity

(CBEST) that became effective in 1983, the California Subject Examination for Teachers (CSET) that became effective in 1983, and the Teaching Performance Assessment (TPA) that became effective in 2008. The Reading Instruction Competency Assessment (RICA) became effective in 1998 for the multiple subjects credential (elementary) and in 2000 for the educational specialist credential. The CBEST is designed to assess basic reading, mathematics, and writing skills. The CSET replaced the PRAXIS II in assessing subject matter competency. The TPA is designed to assess candidates' knowledge, skills, and ability to apply knowledge related to the California Teaching Performance Expectations (TPEs). These assessments are not intended to represent the knowledge base for teaching, or the subject matter knowledge required for teaching. These tests are used as evidence in conjunction with completing an approved teacher preparation program, and recommendation by teacher educators who delivered the program, to determine candidates' readiness for teaching the subjects and grade levels for licensure.

Promising Practices

In one example of a collaborative effort between teacher educators, faculty in the college of arts and sciences, and school practitioners, a secondary English Language Arts (ELA) program was redesigned to meet local needs, state standards, and subject specific assessment for teacher licensure. Recognizing that African American students were the majority of those educated in the program's partner district, team members drew on Tatum's (2005, 2009, 2013) framework for teaching literacy to African American adolescent males. Tatum argued that the literacy curriculum should be empowering for students, which, for African American males included developing curriculum that would allow them to see themselves as part of a *textual lineage,* which Tatum (2009) described as composed of "texts (both literary and nonliterary) that are instrumental in one's human development because of their meaning and significance one has garnered from them" (Tatum, 2009, p. xiv).

The redesigned subject matter course sequence eliminated the required surveys of British literature. Instead, new teachers were required to take two courses from a menu of African American and Latinx literature courses, including *The Civil Rights Movement in African American Literature, From Field Shout to Hip Hop: African American Poetic Traditions,* and *Special Topics in Latina/o Literature.* Unrestricted electives were replaced with requirements for additional upper division writing courses that would aid candidates in understanding how writing and rhetoric can shape and influence social, political, and economic issues in the U.S. Examples of these courses included *Language, Literacy, and Power; The Rhetoric of Public Memory;* and *Women and Rhetoric.* In addition, the traditional English grammar course was supplemented by required coursework in sociolinguistics to help candidates understand the social construction of meaning and power dynamics inherent in language. Working in concert with English department faculty, the School of Education then developed two seminar courses—*Seminar in Teaching and Evaluating Writing* and *English Language Study for Middle and High School Teachers*—that were specifically designed to help teacher candidates synthesize subject matter knowledge from writing, literature, and linguistics courses into curriculum that, guided by Tatum's (2005, 2009, 2013) frameworks, would target the literacy development of the particular students in partner districts. In the end, the team was confident that the redesigned subject matter courses would enable candidates to excel on the Praxis assessment.

The edTPA is an example of a subject specific performance assessment for determining readiness for teaching used by many states where a passing score is required for licensure. This performance assessment is intended to ensure that candidates are minimally prepared to facilitate learning for students at the designated grade level and subject area. This performance assessment has been both contested and praised. Sato (2014) analyzed the edTPA to determine the definition of competent teaching undergirding the assessment. Maintaining that an assessment's conceptualization of teaching is best exemplified by the outcomes required by that assessment. The author compared the outcomes required for a successful performance on the edTPA to those described by seven different scholars whose work has centered on categorization of conceptualizations of teaching. Sato determined that success on the edTPA correlates with a conceptualization of teaching as an executive process of professional decision-making where the teacher establishes "learning goals for his or her students and then orchestrat[es] learning activities for the group of students in an effort to support them toward achieving those goals" (p. 429).

Peck, Gallucci, and Sloan (2010) provide an example of teacher educators engaging with an assessment mandate. These authors described a process for engaging with policy mandates that allowed teacher educators to respond constructively to external policy mandates. Their approach involved developing new forms of engagement and realigning program elements. Opportunities for new forms of engagement included restructuring regular meetings to focus on analyzing samples of candidate submissions for a newly mandated performance assessment. In some cases, candidates were invited to talk through their work and describe challenges with the program. Realignment of program elements involved development of cross-program tools, such as a common lesson plan format, to connect courses and field experiences. The joint engagement of faculty in analyzing candidate work and developing tools to connect courses and field experiences resulted in greater program coherence and collective ownership of the program.

Responding to National Standards and Accreditation

Public education serves the public interest. Thus, the quality of education is of concern to Congress and the federal government. Congress has passed two major legislative initiative focused on improving public schools and teacher preparation, the Elementary and Secondary Education Act (ESEA) 1965 and the Higher Education Act (HEA) 1965 (Figure 8.2).

Congressional Mandates and Requirements

The Elementary and Secondary Education Act (ESEA) of 1965 focused on equal access to quality education. ESEA Title I provided funding for schools and school districts with a high percentage of students from low-income families. The funding was intended to close the achievement gap between low-income students in urban and rural schools and their middle-income peers in reading, writing, and mathematics. Trend data from the National Center for Educational Statistics (NCES) indicates that improvement in the academic achievement of the target population was minimal (NCES, 2013). The 2001 reauthorization of ESEA, known as No Child Left Behind, increased accountability for teachers and students. The new requirements included annual standardized tests to monitor student achievement, schools were accountable for Adequate Yearly Progress (AYP), schools were required to publish annual report cards on students' performance disaggregated by subgroups, schools failing to meet AYP for three consecutive years were required to restructure, and teachers were required to be highly qualified (Paul, 2016). In response to these new standards, many school practitioners narrowed the curriculum and engaged students in rote learning with

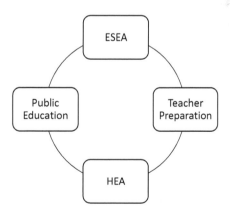

Since 1965, federal legislation has focused on improving P-12 education for underserved students and teacher preparation through funding initiatives in the Elementary and Secondary Education Act (ESEA) and the Higher Education Act (HEA). Outcomes have consistently failed to meet expectations.

FIGURE 8.2 Education in the national interest

hopes of improving standardized test scores. This approach to "teaching to the test" has proven counterproductive.

The Higher Education Act of 1965 (HEA), Title II focused on improving teacher preparation. According to a report of the Congressional Research Service (October 24, 2018):

> Title II of the HEA authorizes grants for improving teacher education programs, strengthening teacher recruitment efforts, and providing training for prospective teachers. This title also includes reporting requirements for states and IHEs regarding the quality of teacher education programs.
>
> *(Hegji, 2018, p. 4)*

HEA funding provides incentives for specific reforms in teacher preparation, including the following:

- Implementing curriculum changes that improve and assess how well prospective teachers develop teaching skills
- Using teaching and learning research so that teachers implement research-based instructional practices and use data to improve classroom instruction
- Developing a high-quality and sustained pre-service clinical education program that includes high-quality mentoring or coaching
- Creating a high-quality induction program for new teachers
- Implementing initiatives that increase compensation for qualified early childhood educators who attain two-year and four-year degrees
- Developing and implementing high-quality professional development for teachers in partner high-need LEAs
- Developing effective mechanisms, which may include alternative routes to certification, to recruit qualified individuals into the teaching profession, and
- Strengthening literacy instruction skills of prospective and new elementary and secondary school teachers.

(Hegji, 2018, p. 7)

States and institutions of higher education receiving HEA funding are required to make annual reports on teacher preparation programs that include specific data such as pass rates of program completers on state required licensure exams and other program quality indicators. States are required to report on licensure requirements, teacher preparation program enrollment data disaggregated by specific demographic characteristics, pass rates disaggregated and ranked by institution, and criteria for identifying low-performing schools of education. The federal requirements for HEA funding and accountability influence state standards and mandates for teacher preparation, and standards and accountability practices for national accreditation agencies.

National Accreditation Standards and Requirements

In comparison to state requirements for teacher preparation program authorization and approval, national standards for accreditation are broader and require more evidence for practices, outcomes, and impact. However, standards for national accreditation are consistent with the focus and accountability requirements of the HEA, ESEA, state requirements and mandates for teacher preparation program authorization and approval. Additionally, the standards of the Council for the Accreditation of Educator Preparation (CAEP) incorporate national standards from InTASC and Specialized Professional Associations (SPAs) in guidance on knowledge and skills for teacher preparation. CAEP has partnerships with 12 SPAs and has a board committee that includes representatives from SPAs that provide advice and guidance.

CAEP has five standards that include:

1.   content and pedagogical knowledge;
2.   clinical partnerships and practice;
3.   candidate quality, recruitment, and selectivity;
4.   program impact; and
5.   provider quality assurance and continuous improvement.

These five standards are supported by two principles for accountability:

- Solid evidence that the provider's graduates are competent and caring educators, and
- There must be solid evidence that the provider's educator staff have the capacity to create a culture of evidence and use it to maintain and enhance the quality of the professional programs they offer.

(http://caepnet.org/standards/introduction)

CAEP has set rigorous standards for evidence supporting the quality of teacher preparation that include validity, reliability, representativeness, cumulativeness, fairness (without bias), robustness, and actionability. The five program standards, the two principles for accountability, and the rigorous standards for evidence combine to provide confirmation that the quality of teacher preparation provided for candidates serves the best interest of all stakeholders and participants at the local, state, and national levels of the society. The findings from the accreditation process reveal program strengths and weakness, and the CAEP standards require evidence for the application of findings for continuous program improvement.

Promising Practices

In a discourse analysis of Australian teacher educators' responses to national standards and mandates, Bourke, Ryan, and Ould (2018) recommend an approach

that involves collaboration and joint inquiry. The authors frame teacher education as a cooperative endeavor among stakeholders in the university and communities of practice, and argue that in responding to mandates, community
"beliefs, values, emotions, context, and traditions [must be] considered so that
shared community understandings can enact policy to practice" (p. 91). Programs
undertaking this approach develop professional learning opportunities for faculty
and build capacity for transformative leadership that enables educators to interpret
and enact national standards and mandates in ways that will maintain program
identity and integrity.

The approaches presented in Chapters 4–7 focused on program explication,
course alignment, clinical experiences, and monitoring and assessing progress towards
competent teaching address state standards for program authorization and approval,
and standards for national accreditation while maintaining program coherence, continuity, and consistency. The program explication process was a collaborative effort
among teacher educators, arts and sciences faculty, and school practitioners for
reviewing and revising the knowledge base and clinical experiences for teacher preparation. This process addressed local needs and standards at the state and national
levels. In the course alignment process, teacher educators collaborated in building on
work in the program explication process to incorporate state and national standards,
including standards from InTASC and Specialized Professional Associations (SPAs),
in developing and revising courses that are meticulously aligned with clinical
experiences. Clinical experiences are purposefully developed to apply the knowledge
base presented in coursework and to incorporate the conceptual elements of the
framework for teacher preparation. Clinical experiences are guided by specifically
designed tools that incorporated epistemic practices and facilitated developing the
related habits of mind associated with competent teaching. The key assessments and
the tools used in guiding advanced clinical experiences monitor and assess progress
towards competent teaching. These tools generate a significant part of the data
required as evidence for national accreditation.

Conclusion

The discussion in this chapter has illuminated the interconnectedness of public
education, teacher preparation, and state and national standards; the impact of
public education on the quality of life in the local community, and the state and
national economy; and legislated incentives for improving teacher preparation
and public education in the interest of the nation. State and national standards
and mandates have not consistently generated responses from teacher educators
and school practitioners that achieve the expected learning outcomes in public
schools. Some teacher educators and school practitioners focus more on meeting
standards and mandates than on improving teaching and teacher preparation.

The discussion in this chapter presented promising practices for meeting standards and mandates while improving teaching and teacher preparation that

include a) opportunities for candidates to collaborate among peers resulting in communities of practice that support continuous professional development and b) partnership agreements between teacher preparation providers and P-12 schools that include collaborative practice-based research addressing persistent challenges and problems. The hope is that our collective efforts in meeting state and national mandates will improve teacher preparation, teaching, and learning outcomes for students as prompted by our commitment to excellence in public service. In the final analysis, the future of the United States is significantly influenced by the quality of education provided for children and youth.

References

Barry, M. N. & Dannenberg, M. (2016). *Out of pocket: The high cost of inadequate high schools and high school student achievement on college affordability.* Washington, DC: Education Reform Now. https://edrefornow.org.

Bourke, T., Ryan, M., Ould, P. (2018). How do teacher educators use professional standards in their practice? *Teaching and Teacher Education, 75,* 83–92.

Constantine, J., Player, D., Silva, T., Hallgren, K., Grider, M., & Deke, J. (February 2009). *An evaluation of teachers trained through different routes to certification.* Washington, DC: Institute of Education Sciences, National Center for Education Evaluation and Regional Assistance. http://ies.ed.gov/ncee/pubs/20094043/pdf/20094043.pdf.

Council of Chief State School Officers (2016). *Interstate New Teacher Assessment and Support Consortium* (INTASC). Washington, DC: Author. http://programs.ccsso.org/projects/interstate_new_teacher_assessment_and_support_consortium/.

Darling-Hammond, L. (2013). Inequality and school resources: What it will take to close the opportunity gap. In P. L. Carter & K. G. Welner (Eds.), *Closing the opportunity gap: What America must do to give every child a chance* (pp. 77–97). New York, NY: Oxford University Press.

Greenberg, J., Walsh, K., & McKee, A. (2014). *Teacher prep review: A review of the nation's teacher preparation programs.* Washington, DC: National Council of Teacher Quality. www.nctq.org/dmsView/Teacher_Prep_Review_2014_Report.

Hegji, A. (2018, October 24). *The Higher Education Act (HEA): A primer.* Washington, DC: Congressional Research Service. https://fas.org/sgp/crs/misc/R43351.pdf.

Hollins, E. R. (2006). Transforming practice in urban schools. *Educational Leadership, 63* (6), 48–52.

Hollins, E. R. (2012). *Learning to teach in urban schools: The transition from preparation to practice.* New York: Routledge Publishers.

Hollins, E. R. (2019). *Teaching to transform urban schools and communities: Powerful pedagogy in practice.* New York: Routledge Publishers.

Hussar, B., Zhang, J., Hein, S., Wang, K., Roberts, A., Cui, J., Smith, M., Bullock Mann, F., Barmer, A., and Dilig, R. (2020). *The Condition of Education 2020 (NCES 2020–2144).* U.S. Department of Education. Washington, DC: National Center for Education Statistics. https://nces.ed.gov/pubsearch/pubsinfo.asp?pubid=2020144.

Institute of Education Sciences: National Center for Education Evaluation and Regional Assistance (2013). *Addressing teacher shortages in disadvantaged schools: Lessons from two Institute of Education Sciences studies.* Washington, DC: Institute of Education Sciences. http://ies.ed.gov/ncee/pubs/20134018/pdf/20134018.pdf.

Jimenez, L., Sargrad, S., Morales, J. & Thompson, M. (2016, September 18). *Remedial education: The cost of catching up.* Washington, DC: Center for Educational Progress. www.americanprogress.org.

Linton, A. S. (2011). *Examining the effects of structured dialogue grounded in socio-culturalism as a tool to facilitate professional development in secondary science* (Unpublished doctoral dissertation). University of Southern California, Los Angeles, California.

McFarland, J., Hussar, B., Zhang, J., Wang, X., Wang, K., Hein, S., Diliberti, M., Forrest Cataldi, E., Bullock Mann, F., and Barmer, A. (2019). *The Condition of Education 2019 (NCES 2019–2144).* US Department of Education. Washington, DC: National Center for Education Statistics. https://nces.ed.gov/pubsearch/pubsinfo.asp?pubid=2019144.

National Center for Education Statistics (2013). *The nation's report card: Trends in academic progress 2012* (NCES 2013 456)., Washington, DC: Institute of Education Sciences, US Department of Education.

New Teacher Project (2012). *The irreplaceables: Understanding the real retention crisis in America's urban schools.* New York: New Teacher Project.

No Child Left Behind Act. Pub. L. 107–110 (2002).

Paul, C. A. (2016). Elementary and Secondary Education Act 1965: Social Welfare History Project. Retrieved from http://socialwelfare.library.vcu.edu/programs/education/elem entary-and-secondary-education-act-of-1965/.

Peck, C. A., Gallucci, C., & Sloan, T. (2010). Negotiating implementation of high-stakes performance assessment policies in teacher education: From compliance to inquiry. *Journal of Teacher Education,* 61 (5), 451–463.

Sato, M. (2014). What is the underlying conception of teaching of the edTPA? *Journal of Teacher Education,* 65 (5), 421–434.

Sutcher, L., Darling-Hammond, L., & Carver-Thomas, D. (2016). *A coming crisis in teaching? Teacher supply, demand, and shortages in the US.* Palo Alto, CA: Learning Policy Institute. https://learningpolicyinstitute.org/product/coming-crisis-teaching.

Southern Regional Education Board (SREB), Teacher Preparation Commission (2018, December). *State policies to improve teacher preparation.* Atlanta, GA: Author. www.sreb. org/publication/state-policies-improve-teacher-preparation.

Tatum, A.W. (2005). *Teaching reading to black adolescent males: Closing the achievement gap.* Portland, ME: Stenhouse.

Tatum, A.W. (2009). *Reading for their life: (Re)building the textual lineages of African American adolescent males.* Portsmouth, NH: Heinemann.

Tatum, A.W. (2013). *Fearless voices: Engaging a new generation of African American adolescent male writers.* New York, NY: Scholastic.

Ujifusa, A. (2019, July 24). Comparing how all 50 states connect schools to the workforce. *Education Week's blogs.* www.edweek.org/ew/section/blogs/index.html?intc=main-topnav.

Warner, C. K. & Hallman, H. L. (2017). A communities of practice approach to field experiences in teacher education. *Brock Education,* 26 (2), 16–33.

Woods, J. R. (2016, May). *Mitigating teacher shortages: Alternative teacher certification.* Denver, CO: Education Commission of the States.

9

EPILOGUE

The information presented in this book is based on a lifetime of scholarship in teacher education—specifically that of Etta Hollins. Her vision of teacher education was built over the course of her professional career. Therefore, the description of my experience with teacher preparation program redesign at one particular university is not meant to imply that my story exemplifies Etta's work, but rather to provide a personal account of what I saw as the transformative power of program redesign at our institution, program redesigned based on her work. I see the key to accomplishing redesign work as being the *enactment of processes* that bring faculty together to think deeply and make decisions about teacher preparation toward effecting change for the benefit of all stakeholders, but primarily for the health, welfare, and futures of the children and youth of our nation.

I had the distinct pleasure of working with Etta Hollins at the University of Missouri–Kansas City while she was Kauffman Endowed Chair for Urban Teacher Education. Our closest collaboration occurred during the time I was chair of the division of Teacher Education and Curriculum Studies. It was a pivotal time for the School of Education as a whole. Two major factors, in combination, created a need for a heightened level of collaborative work, collaboration that would go beyond the norms that had been established as our 'business as usual.' First, there had been a turnover in our school's administrative structure. The dean of the school had left to take a position at another institution and an interim dean was appointed to maintain administrative functions during the search for a new dean. At the same time, deadlines for redesign of teacher preparation programs mandated by the Missouri Department of Elementary and Secondary Education loomed on the horizon.

Faculty work on the redesign of our teacher preparation program, led by the Associate Dean of Teacher Education, occurred during monthly teacher education faculty meetings. To many teacher education faculty, progress toward the goal of a redesigned program seemed elusive. Generally, we did not have the experience necessary to engage as informed participants in the redesign process and could not see how the work we were asked to do would move us forward. The need for redesign, however, was clear. We had explored data from the teacher preparation program and found a lack of coherence and continuity among certification areas. In other words, certification areas within teacher preparation were idiosyncratic. This was particularly evident in results of the mandated tests that were designed by the state to determine candidates' qualification for certification. Our teacher candidates' responses to prompts were not indicative of shared understandings. For example, candidates' use of such terms as *differentiation* and *teaching strategy* produced a wide variety in the quality of their responses and indicated conflicting understandings. The responses were, at the same time, somewhat consistent within each certification area (such as elementary majors or secondary majors). In other words, depending on the area of certification, evidence showed varying degrees of competence for teaching. This variation appeared to be due to a lack of faculty awareness of or agreement on what knowledge, skills, and experiences are required to learn teaching and how knowledge, skills, and experiences combine to make effective teaching possible.

Within the year, the Associate Dean for Teacher Education also left to take an administrative position at another institution. Moreover, the Associate Dean of Teacher Education position was discontinued, leaving us without our customary structure of leadership. Etta Hollins, because of her expertise and experience in teacher education and program design, was asked by the interim dean to lead the teacher education faculty meetings, which included teacher preparation program redesign. Etta agreed to lead the meetings in collaboration with me, the newly appointed chair of the division of Teacher Education and Curriculum Studies, and Connor Warner, a relatively new faculty member whose specific research interest was teacher education.

While most of the teacher education faculty in our division had some form of expertise *related* to teacher education, such as doctoral-level degrees in mathematics education, reading education, or science education, very few of us had actually studied *teacher education*. Most faculty in teacher education had been trained as content area specialists or perhaps 'generalists' in early childhood or elementary education. Considering her expertise and experience working with teacher education faculty in program design or redesign, the interim dean's selection of Etta Hollins to lead faculty in program redesign made perfect sense. Etta would be able to move us beyond our limited views of teacher education to see the bigger picture.

Etta, Connor, and I worked together, as a leadership team, to plan for productive teacher education faculty meetings. The three of us met at least biweekly to strategize on how to lead faculty in such a way that might encourage the development of shared understandings of teacher education and broad faculty participation. All three of us fulfilled countless roles during planning and faculty work sessions, although some delineation of responsibilities emerged. For example, Etta guided our work with her wealth of program design and redesign experience. As division chair, an administrative role, I sent out meeting invitations and attend to other email communication with teacher education faculty. Connor often took the lead in creating example documents that modeled what we had discussed in our planning meetings, so that faculty work on program redesign would not be 'starting from scratch' with every task.

The program redesign work accomplished by teacher education faculty included many of the components described in this book, particularly program explication, course realignment, and development of key assessments. While perhaps our work cannot be described as an ideal collaborative effort, implementation of the processes of redesign had a transformative power. There was an improved level of faculty participation in meetings, particularly evident as additional work meetings were voluntarily attended during the academic school year and extra redesign work done throughout the summer—a time when the majority of faculty were not obligated to university matters. Faculty worked together, shared responsibility for the work—often assisting content area lead faculty in the redesign processes, and expanded their foundational knowledge of teacher education. Additionally, because of transparency of the processes, faculty from other divisions within the school learned more about teacher education, and a few of them contributed to the program redesign.

Perhaps most importantly, evidence of transformative power was not limited to faculty actions and interactions. Since the state's acceptance of the redesigned program, we have seen evidence, through candidates' responses to key assessments, of a greater level of coherence in our teacher preparation program. We have used the results of key assessment (candidates' responses) to evaluate the teacher preparation program and inform efforts toward continuous improvement. While there are no guarantees for the future, I have hope that the processes used for redesign will be sustained and have enduring effects on the quality of the preparation of teacher candidates at the University of Missouri—Kansas City and the quality of educational experiences provided for the children and youth we ultimately serve.

Clare V. Bell
Associate Professor
University of Missouri, Kansas City

INDEX

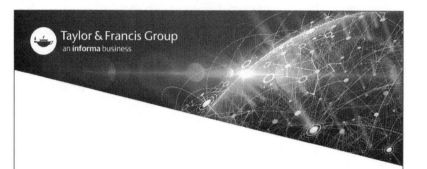